SoJourn

Volume 5, Number 2

A journal devoted to the history, culture, and geography of South Jersey

Winter 2020/21

SoJourn is a collaborative effort. Local historians contribute the articles; Stockton students—in this issue, the editing interns of fall 2020—edit the articles, set the type, and design the layout; the directors of the South Jersey Culture & History Center at Stockton University oversee the publication.

Editors
Sarah E. Augustine, Louis "Bud" Burgess, Nicholas Caputo, Amanda Clark, Sarahjane Hehre, Michael Lorge, Emily Luberto, Emily Montgomery. Additional proofreading by Madison Chris, Amanda Clark, Sierra Estremera, Gabriella Fiorica, Elena Gonzalez, Olivia Harris, Nyzira Lynn, Jay Marachese, Isabella Monacchio, Jonathan Porro, Alison Roemer, James Wynne.

Supervising Editors
Tom Kinsella and Paul W. Schopp

ISSN: 2474-6665
ISBN: 978-1-947889-04-0
A publication of the South Jersey Culture & History Center
at Stockton University
www.stockton.edu/sjchc/

© 2021, the authors, South Jersey Culture & History Center, and Stockton University. All rights reserved.

Filler images, at the conclusion of articles, courtesy of the Paul W. Schopp Collection unless otherwise noted.

To contact SJCHC write:
SJCHC / School of Arts & Humanities
Stockton University
101 Vera King Farris Drive
Galloway, New Jersey
08205

Email:
Thomas.Kinsella@stockton.edu
Paul.Schopp@stockton.edu

About this Issue of *SoJourn*

South Jersey is a fascinating region with a rich cultural history. Comprising the eight southernmost counties of New Jersey, it includes the Pine Barrens with its unique ecosystem and history of natural resource exploitation; the bayshore, with its oystering, fishing, and shipbuilding traditions; agricultural belts that include a number of late nineteenth-century farming communities established by Germans, Italians, and Russian Jews; the many seaside resorts; and urbanized manufacturing centers. *SoJourn* explores and, we believe, helps to preserve these remarkable cultural and physical landscapes.

In the current issue, John W. Lawrence reconsiders the accuracy of Augustine Herrman's 1670 map of Virginia and Maryland, which includes the southwestern portion of New Jersey. Samuel Avery-Quinn details the history of property ownership and use at Sea Breeze along the Delaware Bay, focusing on the second half of the nineteenth century when it was home to the Warner House, a popular excursion destination. We have republished Louis Mounier's short essay about the "Trials and Hardships of Immigrants," which describes a heart-warming reunion of family members in the Alliance Colony on December 31, 1883. Postcard photographs along with details gleaned from contemporary news items describe a catastrophic fire that destroyed the West Jersey & Seashore Railroad's Maurice River Oyster Sheds in 1907. We have continued our republication of stories by Joseph S. Reeves Jr. chronicling life on the Maurice River in the 1940s. Jim Bergmann, noted expert on the life of George Agnew Chamberlain, has described the twentieth-century writings of Chamberlain that use the Pine Barrens as their setting. We hope in future issues to publish selections from Chamberlain's work. Frequent contributor Kenneth W. Able describes the impact of lagoon development on the coastal ecosystem, especially the Ocean County development of Mystic Island. Horace Somes Jr. describes aircraft that might have been sighted over the Pinelands anytime from the 1930s through to today, including the ill-fated Hindenburg, and describes the work of aircraft spotters during the Second World War. This issue also illustrates decoys from the Noyes Museum collection that well-known local carver Gary Giberson has selected and described. It concludes with a brief description of the good work of The South Jersey Horse Rescue in Weekstown.

We are pleased that several of these articles include brief essays or introductions by Stockton students who have taken part in the South Jersey Culture & History Center editing internship. With twenty titles published and nine issues of *SoJourn*, we are proud to show off the work of our student-staffed local history press. We hope you enjoy the issue. Remember, we are always seeking contributions for future publication.

Tom Kinsella

Director
South Jersey Culture & History Center
Stockton University

Map of Contents

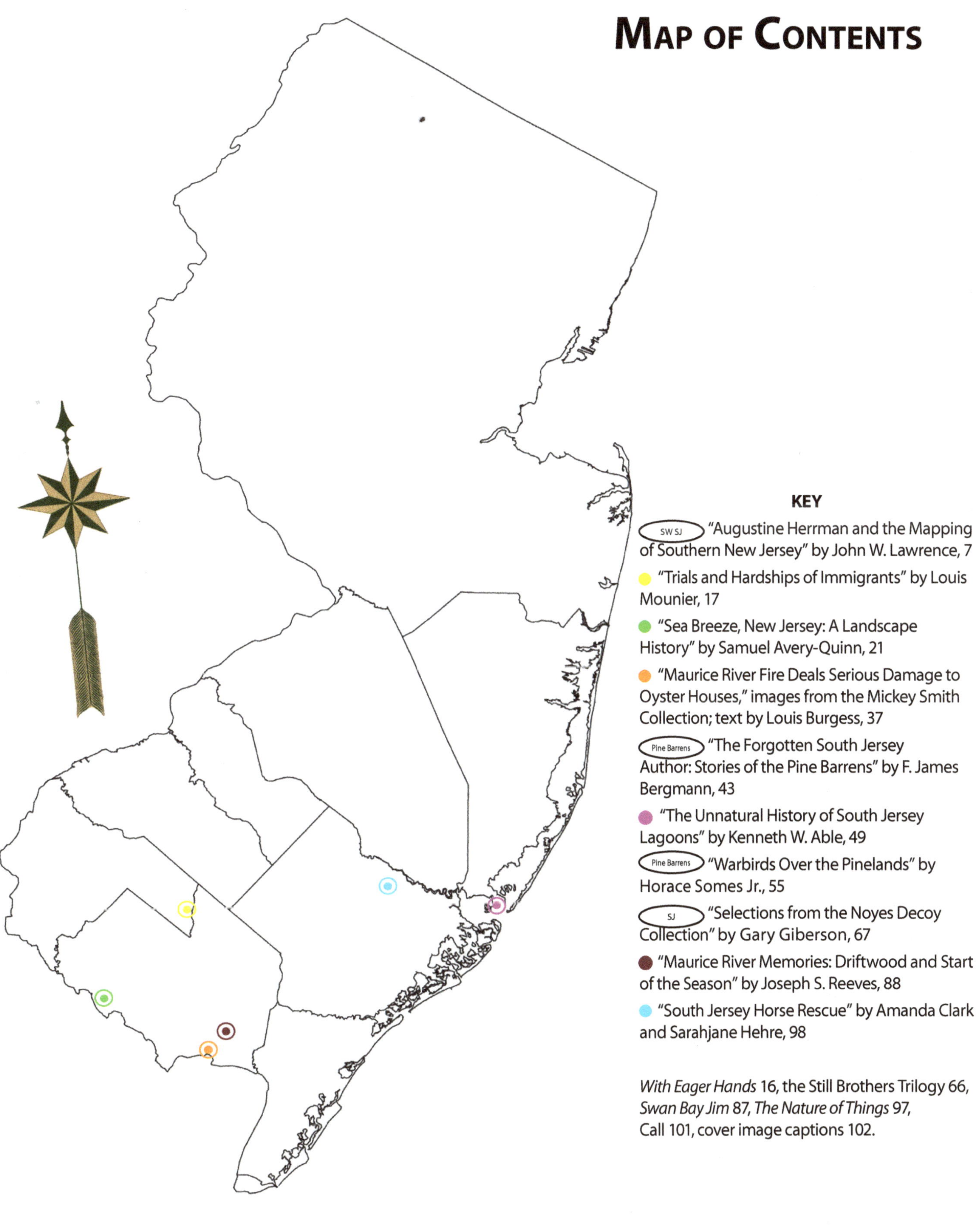

KEY

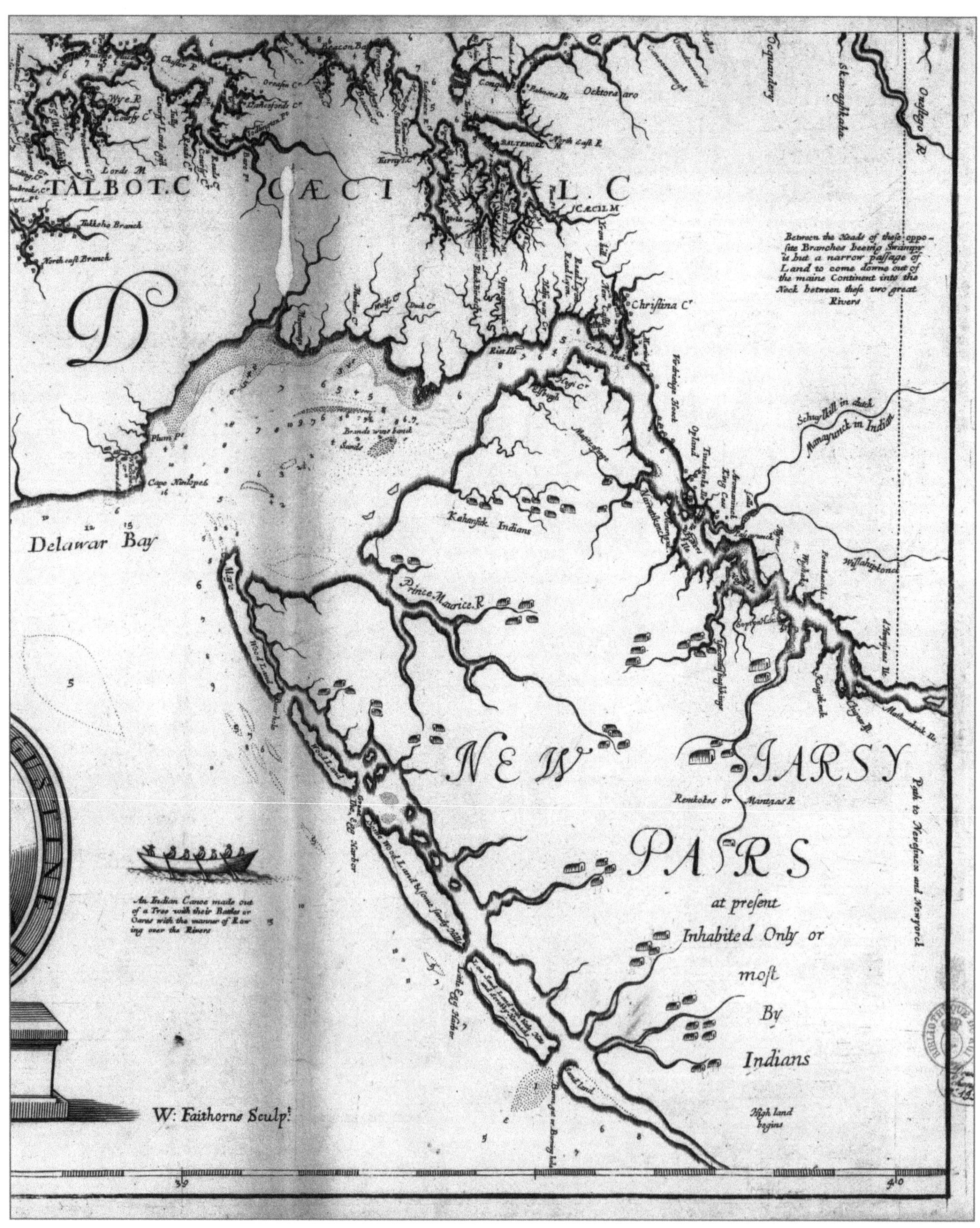

Bottom right quarter panel, New Jersey section, from Augustine Herrman's *Virginia and Maryland As it is Planted and Inhabited this present Year 1670* (London, 1673). Courtesy of the Library of Congress.

Augustine Herrman and the Mapping of Southern New Jersey

John W. Lawrence

For all the multifaceted achievements he realized during his lifetime (1621–1686), Augustine Herrman is virtually unknown in the historiography of New Jersey. Perhaps this is as it should be, since most of his career in the New World oscillated between Dutch colonial New Amsterdam and Lord Baltimore's Maryland colony. Nonetheless, he made a significant, yet generally overlooked, contribution to the early history of the Garden State. Born in Prague, then part of the Roman Catholic Kingdom of Bohemia, at an early age Augustine and his Protestant family removed to the Netherlands due to religious persecution. Little is known of his youth, but in 1644 the 23-year old Herrman immigrated to New Amsterdam as a representative of the Amsterdam-based trading firm of Peter Gabry and Sons.[1]

Once he arrived in New Amsterdam, and over the course of the ensuing 40 years, Herrman greatly expanded the range of his activities beyond those of a simple merchant. In so doing, he assumed the role of a cultural broker or mediator, crossing an array of social, political, cultural and linguistic boundaries. As a New Amsterdam merchant, he traveled extensively throughout the lower Delaware Valley and the Chesapeake region of Maryland, trading in tobacco and other goods, both for Peter Gabry and Sons and for himself. Culturally and diplomatically, he also mediated between the Dutch, English, and Native American worlds. He witnessed land transactions between Dutch settlers and Lenape on the Schuylkill River. At the direction of Peter Stuyvesant, he participated in negotiations between New Amsterdam and New England Puritans over trade and territory. Herrman also belonged to the group known as the "Nine Men," chosen to represent the burghers of New Amsterdam and their interests before the irascible Peter Stuyvesant and the interests of the West India Company. Herrman played his most notable role in 1659 as a diplomat and mediator, when Stuyvesant sent him and Resolved Waldron to negotiate the boundary dispute between the English and Dutch claims to the lower Delaware River and Bay, in land now belonging to Pennsylvania and Delaware.[2]

Traveling to St. Mary's City to negotiate a settlement, Herrman and Waldron argued with their English host, Philip Calvert, over their respective cases for ownership. Calvert displayed a variety of maps depicting the extent of English land possession as a key element to his argument. Herrman adroitly circumvented Calvert's cartographic proof by pointing out the numerous inaccuracies and inconsistencies between the various maps covering the negotiating table. But as any successful mediator knows, Herrman recognized that it was not enough to stymie his host; the moment required him to present a solution to the problem acceptable to all.

Hence, Herrman proposed a new, single, and accurate map of the region be created that could be used as a tool to settle this intercolonial dispute. Of all of Herrman's notable accomplishments, the ten years he dedicated to this endeavor resulted in his most historically significant achievement: *Virginia and Maryland As it is Planted and Inhabited this present Year 1670 Surveyed and Exactly Drawne by the Only Labour and Endeavour of Augustin Herrman Bohemiensis*, published in London in 1673 (Figure 1). The historical significance of this document lies in its precision. It is recognized by cartographers and historians as the first map to accurately depict shorelines, near-shore bathymetry, navigational hazards, and landmass. In accuracy, it far outclassed

Figure 1. Augustine Herrman's *Virginia and Maryland As it is Planted and Inhabited this present Year 1670* (London, 1673). Courtesy of the Library of Congress.

John Smith's popular 1612 map *Virginia Discouvered and Discribed* and Nicolas Visscher's *Novi Belgii Novaque Anglia Nec Non Paris Virginia Tabula,* both of which Herrman's map substantially overlapped in coverage.

As already demonstrated above, the genesis of Herrman's foray into cartography was geopolitical in nature: resolving competing territorial claims necessary to maintain the peace and the profitable inter-colonial trade in peltry, tobacco, lumber, horses, enslaved people, and manufactured items. Colonial competition provided the rationale for creating the map and justification of the royal patronage Herrman received based on the long years of labor it took to create it.[3] What cannot be overlooked is the utility such a map would have for traders and merchants, for whom the waterways served as the highways of the day. For them, detailed information on coastlines and their hazards (shoals, etc.) would be of inestimable value. As historian Christian J. Koot has pointed out, Herrman had a special interest in shorelines, a focus missing from earlier maps. Herrman made much of his fortune while engaged in intercoastal trade and he brought this mercantile perspective to his mapmaking. This is not to suggest that Herrman's creation was particularly self-serving, but only that the map proved a useful tool in supporting the geopolitical interests of its backers, as well as the economic interests of traders and merchants like himself.[4] To that end, regional merchants found the map, with its detailed representations of waterways and locations of colonial plantations, "useful for traders searching for particular places."[5]

With all the painstaking detail found in Herrman's map, it is all the more striking to find the following statement by a contemporary historian: "Herrman chose to leave much of the continent's interior blank, labeling only the colonies and counties and haphazardly indicating some Native American settlements."[6] Knowing that trade with Native Americans provided an important revenue source throughout the North American colonies during the late seventeenth century, why would Herrman denote their locations "haphazardly" if he offered such precision to other features of the landscape? Or, asked in another way, did Herrman indeed depict Native American settlements in a random, or haphazard fashion?

In attempting to answer this question, we employed the most modern of cartographic tools—Geographic Information System (GIS) technology—and compared Herrman's rendering of Native American settlements with the known location of Native American archaeological sites. For manageability, we selected the Rancocas and Pennsauken creek watersheds as our data universe for this comparison (Figure 2). The first step was to overlay Herrman's map with contemporary topographic maps and aerial photography of the region. With due respect given to the remarkable achievement represented by *Virginia and Maryland As it is Planted and Inhabited this present Year 1670*, melding the map with modern GIS layers proved not an easy task and exposed the inevitable errors in Herrman's map projection.[7] That said, however, when we focused our effort on the area of the above-mentioned drainages, the prominent landmarks along the Delaware River that Herrman observed and noted in the 1660s are still viewable today (Figure 3). We then added another data layer containing the location of all currently recorded precontact archaeological sites within the Rancocas and Pennsauken creek drainages (Figure 4).[8]

Before turning our attention to the relationship of these sites to Herrman's recordation of Native American settlements, it is important to point out that the sample of known precontact archaeological sites are not distributed randomly—or haphazardly—across the landscape.[9] We can state this fact with a high level of confidence, having used the ArcGIS HotSpot Analysis tool to test whether the sites are located randomly within the stream drainages or not.[10] The results of the analysis are depicted in Figure 5. In it, we observe that there is at least a 95% chance that the location of an archaeological site falls within one of three loose clusters: 1) along the main stem of the Rancocas Creek; 2) along the South Branch of the Rancocas Creek and headwaters of the Pennsauken Creek and 3) headwaters of the North Branch of the Rancocas Creek.

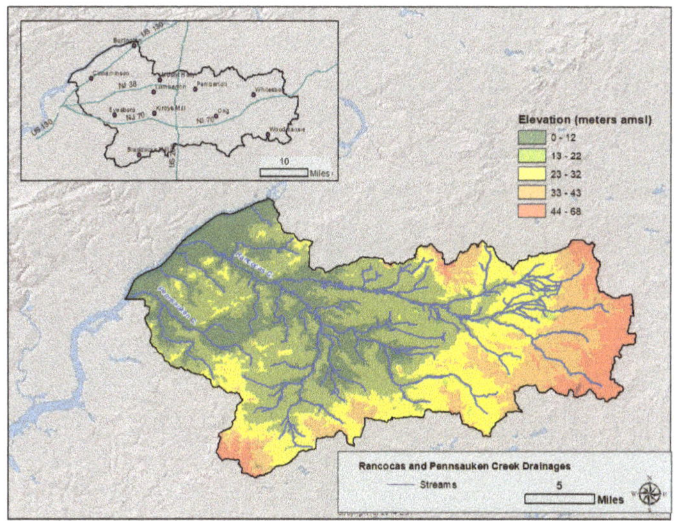

Figure 2. The Rancocas and Pennsauken Creek watersheds.

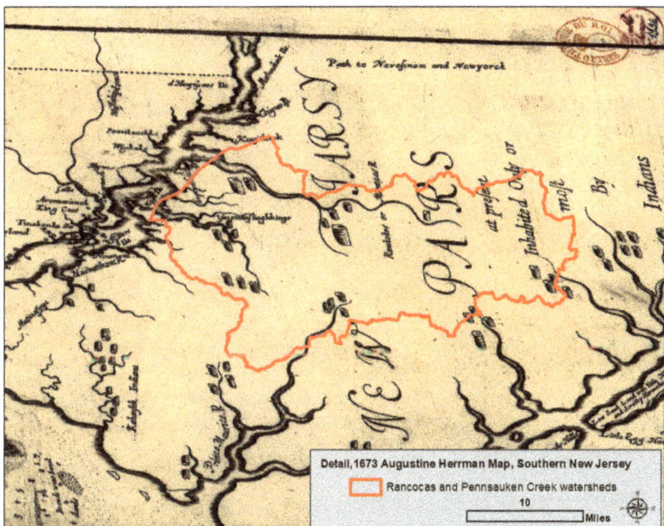

Figure 3. Herrman's rendition of southern New Jersey, with the Rancocas and Pennsauken Creek drainages superimposed.[9]

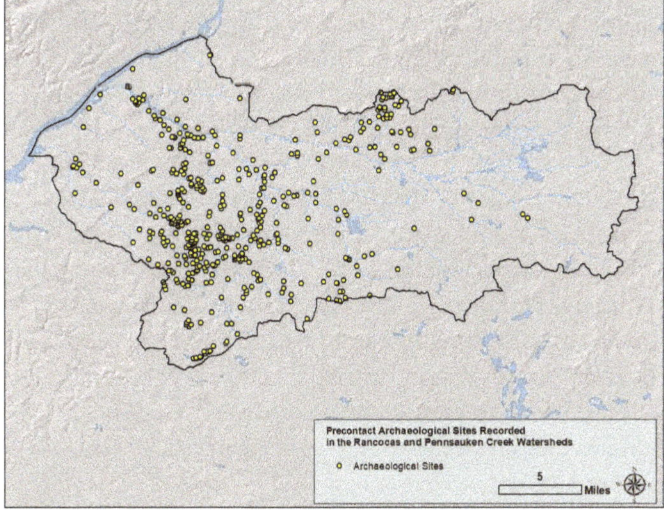

Figure 4. Recorded precontact archaeological sites in the Rancocas and Pennsauken Creek watersheds.

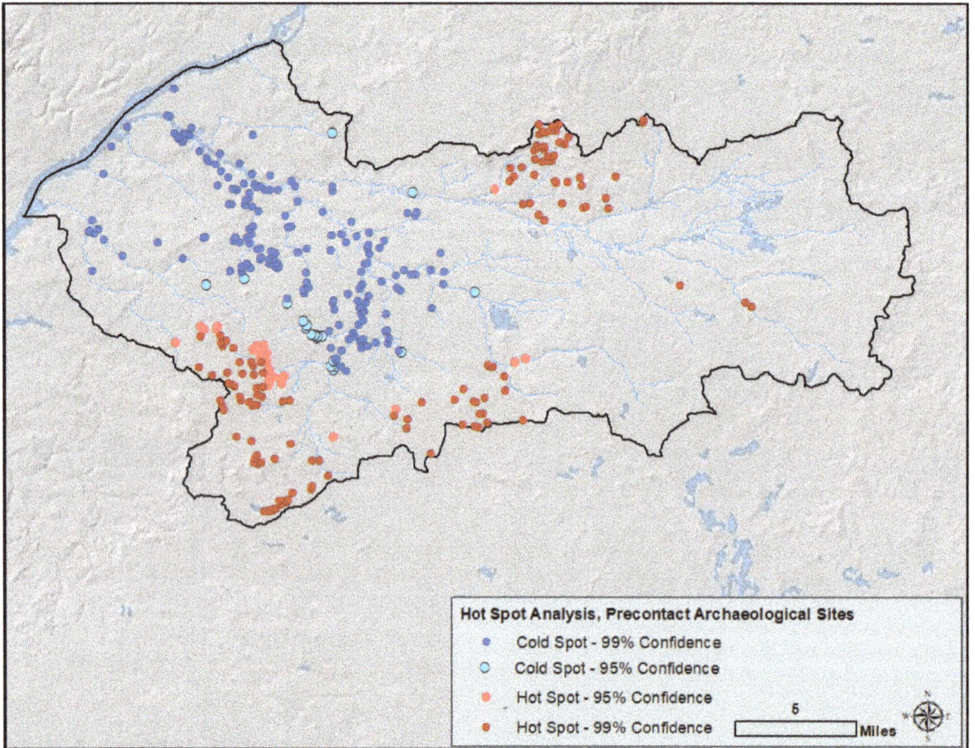

Figure 5. Results of Hot Spot analysis on Pennsauken/Rancocas archaeological sites.

When we examine the distribution of precontact archaeological sites with *Virginia and Maryland As it is Planted and Inhabited this present Year 1670* map, the location where Herrman depicted Native American settlements appears to be more than coincidental. Almost all the settlements—represented by long houses—are situated in those areas identified as most frequently inhabited by Native Americans as documented through archaeological remains. Herrman's long houses are found along the main stem of the Rancocas Creek, at the forks, and near the headwaters of the two branches of the creek (Figure 6). While it must be noted that Herrman's use of the image of the longhouse to illustrate a settlement was a stylistic convention, the evidence strongly suggests that where he chose to depict those settlements was not at all haphazard, but hewed closely to where he knew, by experience, Lenape settlements existed.[11] As a trader, it is entirely reasonable to conclude that Herrman was as intent on illustrating where Native clients were to be found as colonial plantations and the navigational details needed to reach them. To this observation, we should however caution that Herrman's creation is not a roadmap. Herrman's longhouses indicate general areas where Lenape settlements would be found—it is not representational of any individual or actual settlement. As a trader, Herrman would have been aware that Lenape settlements were not permanent in the European sense of the term, but that the indigenous people would move with the seasonal availability of the resources that they depended on for subsistence: towards streams and rivers for the spring shad run, or deeper into the interior to hunt deer in the fall. As discussed below, the larger settlements, occupied for longer periods of time, would be found in those areas with the greatest concentration of wild resources over the course of the year, and the best soil for agriculture. The Forks of the Rancocas provided one such area and this area figures prominently in Herrman's map; the Lenape *sachem* Remokokes may have resided there.[12] Similarly, the longhouse seen along the upper reaches of the North Branch of the Rancocas Creek on Herrman's map may represent the general location of the Lenape settlement *Alumhatta* that was situated near the grounds of contemporary Smithville in 1683.[13]

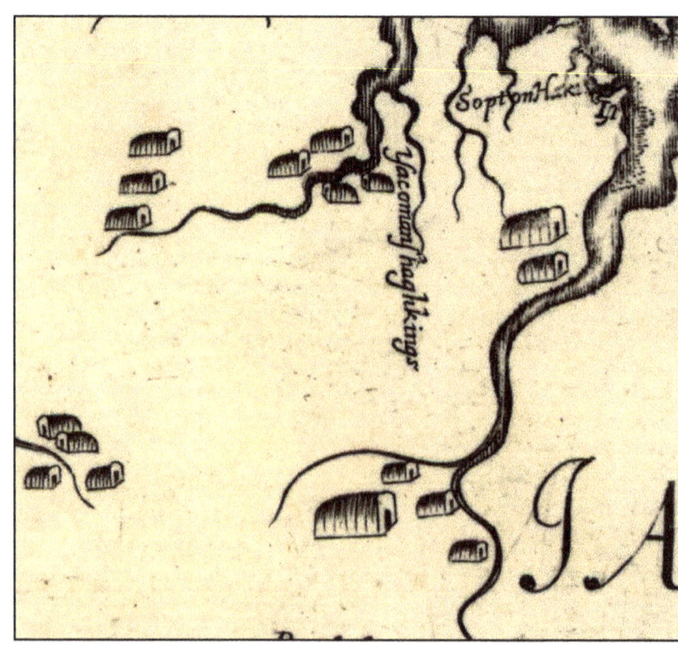

Figure 6. Native American longhouses as drawn by Herrman. These were multi-family dwellings framed with poles and sheathed in tree bark. From Herrman's *Virginia and Maryland As it is Planted . . . .*

Another feature of note on Herrman's map is the fact that it does not depict any Native American settlements along the eastern shore of the Delaware River and none west of the river. Students of the region have interpreted this absence of settlement to be the result of conflict between the Lenape and the neighboring Susquehannock to the west.[14] During the early seventeenth century, Susquehannock raiding parties harassed the Lenape, who fled into the interior of southern New Jersey.[15] The Dutch patroon David De Vries graphically recounted these events when he explored the lower Delaware River in early 1633:

> The next day, the 13th [of January, 1633], three Indians of the Armewamen [a band of the Lenape] came, who were at the yacht before. They told us that they were fugitives—that the Minquas [Susquehannock] had killed some of their people, and they had escaped. They had been plundered of all their corn, their houses had been burnt, and they had escaped in great want, compelled to be content with what they could find in the woods. . . . The main body of their people lying about five or six hours' journey distant, with their wives and children. They told us also, that the Minquas had killed ninety men of the Sankiekens [another Lenape band].[16]

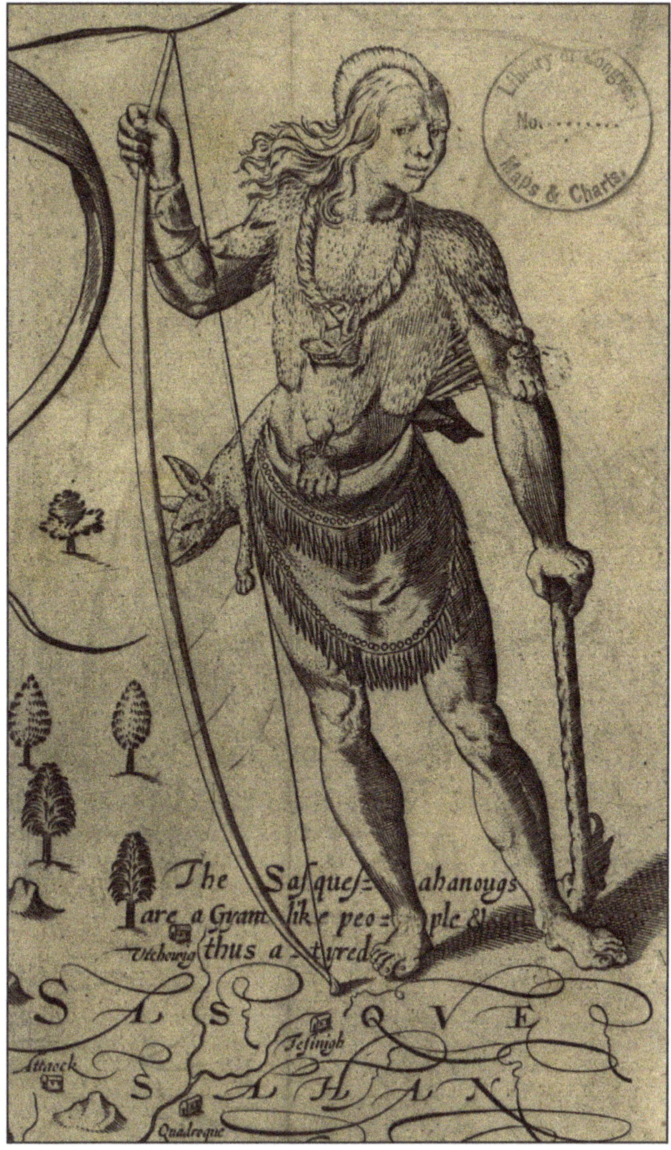

Figure 7. Susquehannock warrior, as depicted in 1624. From *Virginia*. Engraved by William Hole, London, 1624. Courtesy of the Library of Congress.

There is no doubt that the Lenape were displaced from their known habitation sites along the region's waterways to escape the Susquehannock raiders (Figure 7). And while the event described by De Vries in 1633 is attributed to the Susquehannock's desire to dominate trade with Europeans along the Delaware River, it is more than likely that similar displacements had occurred in the precontact past, with no input from European outsiders.

However, if we return to the archaeological site data, we can observe that the pattern of Native American settlement favoring the middle reaches of the Rancocas and Pennsauken creeks has considerable time depth (Figure 8). In fact, Native American settlement in these stream drainages has been remarkably stable for the past 10,000 years of Native American occupation.[17] Each of the three areas favored for settlement hosted occupation at least since Early Archaic Period, or 8000 BCE. Therefore, while inter-tribal conflict was undoubtedly a reality before the arrival of Europeans, it seems an insufficient explanation for the observable pattern of settlement. Other factors likely played a role for where Native Americans chose to live in this area.

Confident that the location of the archaeological sites in the sample are not random, and that the preference for certain areas has considerable time-depth, what factor(s) might be responsible for the observed preference for where Native American's chose to settle? For the majority of the precontact past, Native American societies in the mid-Atlantic region—as elsewhere in the northeast—practiced a hunter/gatherer way of life, in which they hunted and gathered wild plants and animals and fished as these food sources became seasonally available. Archaeological evidence suggests that Native Americans in the region began growing their own food (principally maize, beans, and squashes) circa A.D. 1000, but that food production never fully supplanted hunting, gathering, and fishing as a source of food and other goods necessary for survival. Specialists have debated the nature of Lenape economics at the time of European contact, with some arguing for the primacy of fishing,[18] while others have suggested that the Lenape exercised dual economy, where they could alternate between the hunting and gathering of wild resources and agriculture, when, where, and as needed.[19] Regardless, there is general agreement that the Lenape whom Herrman encountered practiced a generalized economy based on the seasonal availability of wild plants and animals, supplemented with agriculture.

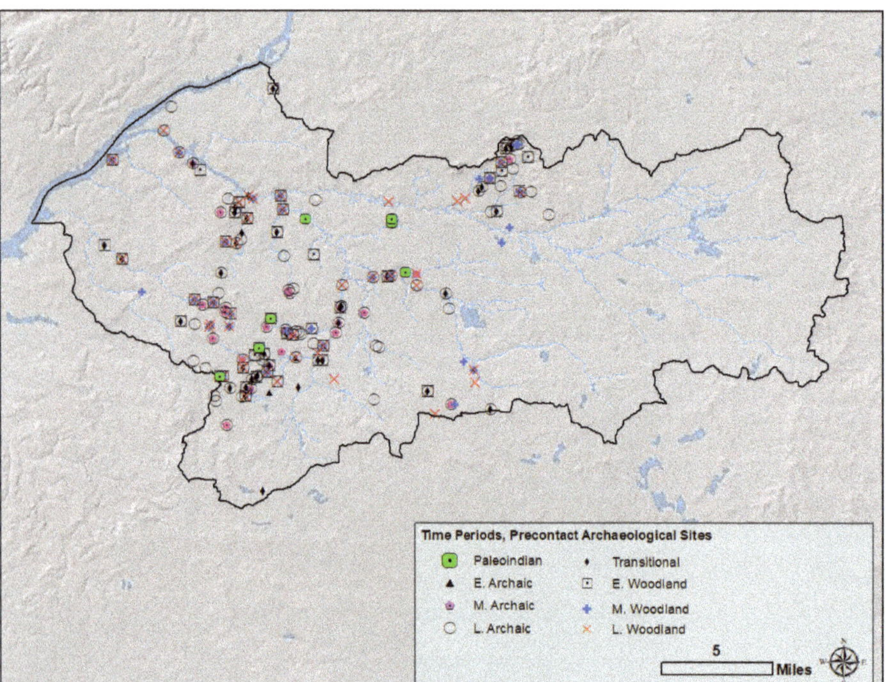

Figure 8. Dated precontact sites in the Rancocas/Pennsauken Creek drainages.

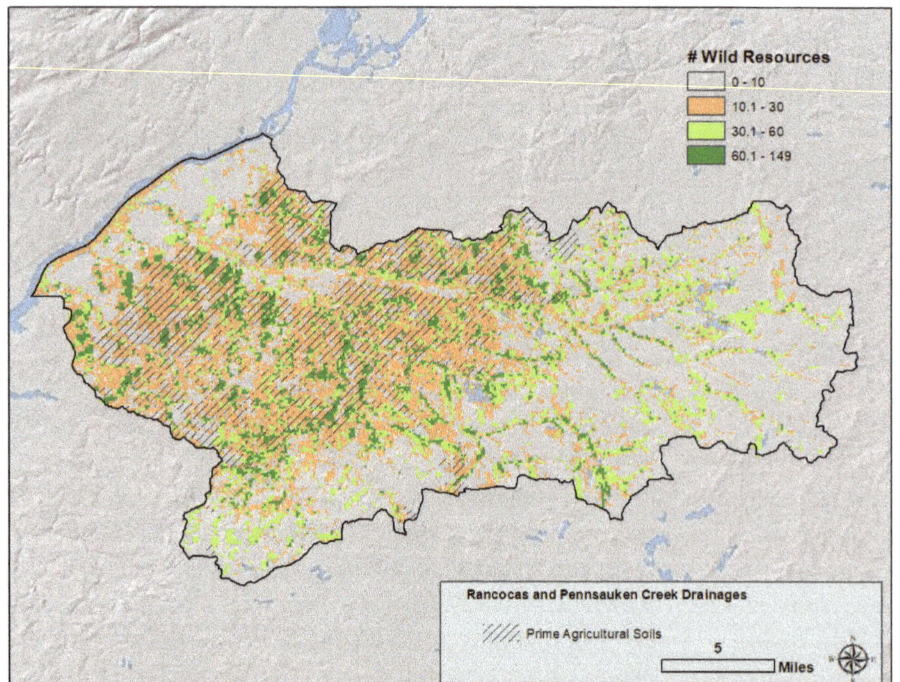

Figure 9. Distribution of wild resources and prime agricultural land in the Rancocas/ Pennsauken watersheds.

In temperate regions such as the mid-Atlantic, the hunter/gatherers' search for food occurred within a *seasonal round*, where people either traveled to, or relocated to different areas within their territory based on where resources can be found at a given season of the year. For example, the native inhabitants of the Rancocas/Pennsauken valleys would have camped near the Delaware River or principal streams to gather shad and other anadromous fish[20] in the early spring and move into the hilly interior in the fall to hunt.

Knowing this, we examined the relationship between archaeological sites in our sample and the distribution of wild plants and economically important animals, e.g., shad and deer, to see whether concentrations of these resources within the region could be responsible for the non-random location of archaeological sites.[21] In addition to the distribution of wild plant and animal species through each season of the year, we examined the distribution of the soils with the highest productivity, which would have been attractive for agriculture.[22]

Our comparative analysis was run for each season of the year (and for agricultural soils), but for simplicity's sake, Figure 9 combines them to illustrate the aggregate total of wild resources that could be found over the course of the entire year, plus the areas of prime agricultural land. Interestingly, the land bordering the Delaware River is not prime farmland; rather, productive land lies in the mid-creek drainage area, between the Delaware

River terraces to the west and the drier sandy Pinelands to the east. This observation holds equally well for wild resources: it is the mid-drainage area that contains the greatest number of wild plants and animals exploited by Native Americans, although those resources are generally spread in a wide band across that area.

When looking at the relationship of precontact archaeological sites and areas containing the highest concentration of seasonal resources (or agricultural land), over 80% of the archaeological sites can be associated with either one or more of the wild resource seasons and/or prime agricultural soils (Table 1).[23]

Table 1. Pennsauken/Rancocas precontact archaeological sites resource associations.

Season	Dec - April	April - July	July - Oct	Oct - Dec	Ag-Soils*	No assoc
# Sites	113	215	84	46	325	86
% of Sites	24.67	46.94	18.34	10.04	70.96	18.78

* prime agricultural soils

As demonstrated, the presence of good soils and wild resources available in the spring and early summer have the greatest number of associated sites. We also note that over 50% of the sites can be associated with two or more resource seasons (Table 2).[24] This could be interpreted to mean that Native Americans chose their settlements carefully to maximize the amount of time during the year that they could exploit resources in the area. We can also speculate that settlements associated with only one resource season existed for the temporary exploitation of the resources available during that season. Conversely, the few (nine in total) sites associated with all available resources may represent permanent settlements, occupied on a year-round basis. Archaeological investigations would be needed to confirm these suppositions.

Table 2. Number of seasons and agricultural soils associated with individual sites.

# Resource Seasons/ Ag soils	0	1	2	3	4	5
# Sites	86	131	99	107	22	9
% Sites	18.78	28.60	21.62	23.36	4.80	1.97

Conclusions

Much to our loss, any documentation that Augustine Herrman might have prepared to describe or explain the methods he used to compile his remarkably detailed map are not available to researchers today. Nevertheless, we can now admire that effort even more, recognizing that not only did he take extreme pains with details of the physical environment, but with the cultural environment as well. This is a fact that historians have generally missed as they have focused on the geopolitical and economic context of the map's creation. It remains to be seen whether the coincidence of archaeological sites and Herrman's long houses is replicated in other stream valleys of southern New Jersey and beyond, and whether the association of archaeological sites and natural resources we see in the Rancocas/Pennsauken drainages is found elsewhere as well. If this indeed proves to be the case, Herrman's *Virginia and Maryland As it is Planted and Inhabited this present Year 1670* map deserves to be considered an ethnohistoric document of the first order.

Bibliography

Barnes, Carol. "Subsistence and Social Organization of the Delaware Indians; 1600 A.D." *Bulletin of the Philadelphia Anthropological Society* 20, no. 1 (1968):15–29.

Becker, Marshall. "Anadromous Fish and the Lenape." *Pennsylvania Archaeologist* 76 (2006): 28–40.

__________. "Lenape Culture History: The Transition of 1660 and its Implications for the Archaeology of the Final Phase of the Late Woodland Period." *Journal of Middle Atlantic Archaeology* 27 (2011): 53–72.

Bolger, William. *Smithville: The Result of Enterprise.* Mount Holly, NJ: The Burlington County Cultural and Historical Commission, 1980.

DeVries, David. "Voyages from Holland to American, A.D., 1632 to 1644." *Collections of the New York Historical Society.* Section Series III, part I. Henry C. Murphy, translator. New York, NY: D. Appleton and Company, , 1857.

Heck, Earl L. W. *Augustine Herrman: Beginner of the Virginia Tobacco Trade Merchant of New Amsterdam and First Lord of Bohemia Manor in Maryland.* Richmond, VA: The William Byrd Press, 1941.

Herrman, Augustine and Thomas Withinbrook. *Virginia and Maryland as It Is Planted and Inhabited this present Year 1670 Surveyed and Exactly Drawne by the Only Labour and Endeavour of*

Augustin Herrman Bohemiensis. London, 1673. https://www.loc.gov/resource/g3880.ct000766/?r=-0.41,0.001,1.499,0.738,0.

Koot, Christian J. "The Merchant, the Map, and Empire: Augustine Herrman's Chesapeake and Interimperial Trade." *The William and Mary Quarterly* 67, no. 4 (2010): 603–44.

Schopp, Paul W. "The Forks of the Rancocas: A History." Typescript report prepared for the Burlington County Board of Chosen Freeholders, Burlington County Division of Parks, Eastampton, NJ, 2013.

Smith, John. *Virginia.* Engraved by William Hole, London, 1624. https://www.loc.gov/resource/g3880.ct000377/?r=-0.325,-0.017,1.74,0.856,0.

Soderlund, Jean R. *Lenape Country.* Philadelphia: University of Pennsylvania Press, 2015.

Stephonitis, L. and W. Mitchell. "Subsistence Settlement Strategies: A Predictive Model for the Upper Susquehanna River Valley. I-88 Archaeological Project PIN 9357.08 and PIN 9357.12 Mitigation Report." Report prepared by the Public Archaeology Facility, Statue University of New York at Binghamton for the New York State Education Department, Albany, New York, NY, 1978.

Versaggi, Nina M. "Hunter-Gatherer Settlement Models and the Archaeological Record: A Test Case from the Upper Susquehanna Valley of New York." Typescript Ph.D. Dissertation, State University of New York, Binghamton, New York, 1987.

Visscher, Nicolaes. *Novi Belgii Novaque Anglia: nec non partis Virginiae tabula multis in locis emendata.* Amsterdam?, 1685. https://www.loc.gov/item/97683561/.

Yong, Thomas. "Relations of Capitan Thomas Yong, 1634." *Narratives of Early Pennsylvania West New Jersey and Delaware 1630-1707.* Albert Cook Myers, editor. New York: Charles Scribner's Sons, 1912.

Acknowledgment

The author would like to thank several individuals for their kindly yet accurate comments on earlier drafts of this article: Ms. Elizabeth Rival of FEMA, Mr. John (Jack) Cresson of the firm R. Alan Mounier, and Dr. Jean Soderlund of Lehigh University. I would also like to thank Paul W. Schopp of Stockton University for his continued encouragement to see this project through to completion.

About the Author

John Lawrence is a former resident of Burlington City and currently serves as an Archaeologist for the Federal Emergency Management Administration. He has practiced archaeological and historical investigations across the mid-Atlantic states over the past thirty years. His professional experience has included original research into the history and prehistory of South Jersey, in which he holds a special interest in historic farmsteads and farm life.

Endnotes

1 E. Heck, *Augustine Herrman* (Richmond: The William Byrd Press, 1941), 11.

2 C. Koot, "The Merchant, the Map, and Empire: Augustine Herrman's Chesapeake and Interimperial Trade," *The William and Mary Quarterly* 67, no. 4 (2010), 604–605, 610.

3 For his efforts, the Calverts awarded Herrman formal trading and property rights in the English colony and 4,000 acres on the Bohemia River in Cecil County, Maryland. Herrman acquired an additional 1,000 acres and he used the assembled acreage to create his *Bohemia Manor*, naming himself *Lord of Bohemia Manor*. The Dutch did not extend any patronage to Herrman for his effort; in fact, he was in the process of becoming a denizen of Maryland during the decade he took to create his map. Heck, *Augustine Herrman*, 62–63.

4 Unfortunately, we know nothing about how Herrman created his map; if he created a diary of his journey, or prepared drafts of the map, or had other records reflecting his method or source materials for his map, none of these items are available to the modern historian. Regardless, we can assume that his extensive travels throughout the region provided the direct observation and measurements on which the precision of his map depended.

5 C. Koot, "The Merchant, the Map, and Empire," 620.

6 Ibid., 619.

7 For example, Herrman misjudged the severity of the northeastward bend in the Delaware River in the vicinity of Wilmington, Delaware.

8 Dr. Gregory Lattanzi of the New Jersey State Museum generously provided the locational information of these sites, to which the author is indebted. The total number of recorded precontact sites used in this analysis is 548, of which 277 have occupation dates.

9 There is a notable lack of recorded sites at the eastern end of the watershed, which consists of Pinelands vegetation. In relative terms, impoverished of resources in comparison to the coastal plains, this paucity of sites is perhaps not surprising. The lack of precontact sites bordering the Delaware River is more surprising, until we consider the degree of historic development between the river and the I-295 corridor, which has both destroyed sites, as well as

made the search for them nearly impossible.

10 The tool determines the probability (*P*) of whether the distribution of sites (or whatever phenomenon is being studied) is random or not and returns P values of 90%, 95% 99%. In other words, that there is a 90, 95, or 99 percent probability that the distribution is non-random. The statistic defines these as either "hot" or "cold" depending on what tail of the normal curve the sample item falls.

11 There is no ethnohistoric evidence that Native Americans constructed longhouses in southern New Jersey. To date, archaeological evidence is equivocal; living floors approximating the dimensions of Iroquois longhouses have been documented in the area, but they are not accompanied with evidence of house structures. Longhouse structures were common to Tribal Nations to the north and south of southern New Jersey and would have been immediately recognizable to Herrman's contemporaries. Interestingly, Herrman's biographer, Earl Heck, was mystified by the use of this symbol, which he likened to "a curious diagram, resembling a covered wagon without the wheels and body." Heck, *Augustine Herrman*, 66.

12 Paul W. Schopp, "The Forks of the Rancocas: A History," typescript report, 2013, iii.

13 Confirmation for the existence of this settlement appears in a 1683 deed for 500 acres of land, including a portion on which Smithville would eventually be built. W. Bolger, *Smithville: The Result of Enterprise* (Mount Holly: Burlington County Cultural and Historical Commission, 1980), 3.

14 J. Soderlund, *Lenape Country* (Philadelphia: University of Pennsylvania Press, 2015), 15–17. Soderlund points out (personal communication) that there were in fact Lenape settlements along the west side of the Delaware River during the seventeenth century that are not depicted on Herrman's map, which is true. The point being made here is that the banks of the Delaware were not a focus of precontact settlement.

15 D. DeVries, "Voyages from Holland to American, A.D., 1632 to 1644," *Collections of the New York Historical Society* (New York: D. Appleton and Company, 1857); Thomas Yong, "Relations of Capitan Thomas Yong, 1634" *Narratives of Early Pennsylvania West New Jersey and Delaware 1630–1707* (New York: Charles Scribner's Sons, 1912), 38–41.

16 DeVries, "Voyages from Holland to American," 30.

17 During the Early Archaic period (8000–6000 BCE), there is an obvious preference for the headwaters of the Rancocas Creek's South Branch and Pennsauken Creek. The preceding Paleoindian period also illustrates this preference, but Paleoindian sites are also recorded along the main stem of the Rancocas Creek.

18 M. Becker, "Anadromous Fish and the Lenape," *Pennsylvania Archaeologist* 76 (2006), 28–40. M. Becker, "Lenape Culture History: The Transition of 1660 and its Implications for the Archaeology of the Final Phase of the Late Woodland Period" *Journal of Middle Atlantic Archaeology* 27 (2011), 53–72.

19 C. Barnes, "Subsistence and Social Organization of the Delaware Indians; 1600 AD," *Bulletin of the Philadelphia Anthropological Society* 20, no. 1, 19.

20 Species that live in the ocean but travel in large numbers upstream in fresh water to spawn in the spring (e.g., shad, sturgeon, alewife). These were an important food source for the Native Americans, as well as for Europeans until overharvesting and water pollution decimated the fish populations, which are fortunately now returning.

21 Over 100 species used; based on data collected and interpreted by Stephonitis and Mitchell (1978) and as presented in Versaggi (1987).

22 For the purpose of this analysis, our identification of agricultural soils in the Rancocas/Pennsauken drainage is defined solely on soil types classified by the USDA as "prime farmland."

23 Sites are considered associated with a specific resource season if the site falls within 300 meters of any area of highest resource concentration for that season; therefore, sites can be associated with more than one resource season. Sites are associated with food production if the site falls within the boundaries of a soil type defined as prime farmland by the USDA.

24 This presence of sites associated with more than one resource season explains why the percentage of sites in Table 2 totals more than 100.

Albertine Senske's long-awaited biography of Elizabeth White is published. *With Eager Hands* details the life of Elizabeth Coleman White (1871–1954), an extraordinary woman and one of New Jersey's shining stars. Horticulturist, conservationist, and social advocate, Elizabeth was a powerful voice in The American Cranberry Growers' Association. With Frederick V. Coville, she cultivated the modern blueberry. Her contributions to improving social conditions and agricultural practices in New Jersey were outstanding. Her life's work and that of other family members is preserved at Whitesbog Village, past headquarters of Joseph J. White, Inc., once the largest cranberry farm in New Jersey. Albertine Senske presents the details of Elizabeth's rich and consequential life with infectious passion.

Available at Whitesbog, Second Time Books in Mount Laurel, and Amazon.com.
ISBN: 978-1-947889-02-6 $15.95

Trials and Hardships of Immigrants

Louis Mounier

Louis Mounier (1852–1937), a humane and cultured painter from France, appears to have immigrated to the United States in 1873 and later accepted a position helping to expand the cultural horizons of Russian Jews who settled in the farming colonies of South Jersey, in particular Alliance, Carmel, and Rosenhayn. In 1901, the Jewish Agricultural and Industrial Aid Society employed Mounier to encourage adult education and training. He brought to bear an extensive knowledge and practice of the arts and history. With Mounier's help, the colonists expanded libraries, built social halls, and implemented extensive programs of lectures and music.

Mounier studied painting and sculpture at the Association Philotechnique in Paris where he received several prizes for his work. After his accomplishments in Paris, Mounier traveled to London, where he learned and mastered English. From 1878–1894, Mounier directed an art school in New York City where he pioneered the training of aspiring painters to join the developing art industry. Later Mounier moved to Vineland, New Jersey, where he was appointed the Director of Educational Work in the Colonies. His primary goal was to enhance community life by sharing knowledge and artistic appreciation throughout the colonies.

Mounier's compassion for the Jewish immigrant community is evident in the following essay, written in 1913 and later published in The Vineland Historical Magazine *in 1933. In touching detail, Mounier describes the arrival of Yenta Kleinfeld and her three children at the Bradway train station, outside of Vineland. They were on the final leg of the arduous journey from Russia to join Joseph Kleinfeld, who had arrived a year earlier in the nascent Alliance farming colony. On this dark, cold and rainy evening, December 31, 1883, their arrival was unexpected. Mounier narrates the ultimately happy reunion.*

In the afternoon of Monday, December 31st, 1883, snow was falling over all of the Eastern States north of Philadelphia. In the southern part of New Jersey, the temperature being just above the freezing point, the precipitation took the form of rain, a glacial rain, enough so as to cause it to remain on the ground almost as slush. A more dreary day could not be imagined. Snow would have lent its purity of tone, its mellowness, its relative warmth, as well as its beautifying curves, over every sharp edged thing or feature, and would not have drenched or soaked everything it touched, as did this driving, penetrating, chilling, rain. This was an instance of what a mere degree of temperature may do. At 31: beauty, softness, comfort; at 32: rain, slush, wet, bedraggled garments; depression, and misery.

Southern New Jersey, or South Jersey, as it is commonly called, is, and has been advertised, as well-nigh snowless; but while this is partly true, at times, its chilly, dreary, damp, and raw days, when rain seems colder than ice, make one often wish for a carpet of beautiful snow.

Bradway station (later on called Norma), where the events related in this sketch occurred, was situated three and a half miles west of Vineland, on the Central Railroad of New Jersey, just about at the center of the southernmost part of the State, in what used to be called the "Pine Belt" and "The Barrens," which originally were covered with coarse scrub-pines, but in that time were grown over mostly with black, red, scrub, worm-eaten, oak trees.

There was then but one house within a stone's throw of the station. To the northward, another house near a saw mill (a rustic, and even then, dilapidated affair), and a couple of farm houses in the clearing constituted the "village."

Self portrait by Louis Mounier, Director of Educational Work in the Colonies. Courtesy of R. Alan Mounier.

Trials and Hardships of Immigrants

There were two trains daily: one in the morning, the other scheduled to reach the place at about six o'clock (or an hour earlier than it is supposed to do at present). When all went tolerably well, this train was usually only half an hour late.

On that last afternoon of the year 1883, rain was at its worst. It was pitilessly falling, not in torrents, but steadily and ceaselessly. There was enough of a Northeast wind to be distinctly audible, as it blew through the branches of the trees, the needles of the native pines, and the sered but tenacious leaves of the white and scrub oaks.

Barring this howling of the wind through the bleak forest, there was an impressive silence. It seemed that the day was to end, as the year was to close, with an absolute absence of human activities, of human noises, of human presence.

As the long twilight of December was imperceptibly creeping in, the dismal dreariness increased, and night alone could not possibly lessen in some degree, this depressing phase of Nature's unhappy moments.

On that night, it was almost seven o'clock when the train stopped at the station (then only a flag one, composed of a small platform but slightly raised above the ground).

Four passengers alighted: one poor woman and her three children. The night was pitch dark, particularly for those who had been in that two-car train, though to be sure, it was not the great brilliancy of its lights that blinded their eyes. When the conductor helped the woman to jump the last step, she felt as though she were falling into a bottomless chasm. However, the instant her feet touched the boards of that platform she became reassured. Then she heard the brakeman throw down a couple of big bundles, which by the dull thump one made as it struck the boards, betrayed the mattresses that immigrants usually bring with them, while the other, on the contrary, rattled and clashed, indicating cooking and household utensils brought over with much trouble for economy's sake.

No sooner had these been thrown down than the locomotive bell changed its coarse tones, breaking still more the silence of the night, and the train resumed its desultory gait, and disappeared gradually into the inky darkness of the night, its red rear-lights becoming fainter and fainter, more so by the rain than by the distance.

It was so dark, even when the train light had vanished away and the eyes of the poor passengers had had time to grow accustomed to the night, that the trees did not so much as make an outline against the sky.

They now felt that some mistake had been made, for there was not a soul to greet them, no welcome sound, no foot-steps, no voices, no horse-hoofs' patter, which would have been so gladly heard.

The distressed quartet peered into the blackness of the night, but saw no signs of habitation. They were getting wetter every minute, though they could not see the rain. They had been dropped there on a platform which they could not even perceive. They groped all around them for a shelter of some kind, but as they reached its edge, were fearful of stepping off, those ten or twelve inches seeming an abyss to them, for that foot of space was invincible, and in their plight they retained no other feelings in their disconsolate hearts than those of despair.

They now missed the companionship of the few passengers who were on the train, and, though they had not said as much as one word to any of them and had not been noticed nor spoken to, when that train and its human crew and cargo and its lights became lost to their sight, they experienced an inexpressible feeling of forsaken loneliness.

They waited and waited, becoming more and more soaked, more and more chilled. Not a board to creep under! Nothing but a miserable shawl which the woman had over her head, and which she tried to share with the two youngest children. In less than a half hour this garment was wet through, and the rain was now running down their backs. They waited thus, and no one came. They were not only half frozen, but faint from want of food.

By this time they could dimly see to the northward a faint ray of light. This glimmer was seen only from some places on the platform, for, between it and this feeble light which was in the kitchen of the Bradway farmstead, there was a chicken yard and coops.

They exchanged a few words in a strange and uncouth tongue. The children were crying softly and pitiably, and the poor woman was now silent and disconsolate. Her tears by this time had ceased flowing, but her intense and mute despair, the spasmodic wringing of her hands, would have been heartrending to behold, had there been enough light to reveal them.

At all costs they must do something. Seeing the uselessness of waiting any longer, they felt their way, guided by that glimmering light, and, wading through the mud—half tumbling into holes, bumping against a fence, now and then losing sight of that dim guiding star which grew scarcely brighter as they neared it—they, the four of them, finally reached the farmhouse without having been heard. They timidly rapped at the door and with throbbing hearts and countenances so pitiful that they haunted the owner of that farm to his dying day, they at last stood before human beings.

Words were exchanged by both parties, but they expressed nothing to the addressed party; they were both unintelligible, save for an unmistakable distress on one side, and kindliness on the other. The wanderers were using the Yiddish jargon, the Bradways the English language.

However Mr. Bradway soon saw the situation; these people must be taken to their relatives, two and a half miles away, to Alliance, the new settlement of Russian Jews. The state of the roads and the weather, as well as the lateness of the hour now that the quartet had been warmed and partly dried, prompted him to proffer food and shelter for the night; but they either did not understand him, or manifested unmistakingly their desire to be led to their husband and father.

Mr. Bradway had only an open farm wagon on which to place the four people, and their belongings which he had fetched from the platform while they were warming themselves around the kitchen stove. The dripping bundles on one end of the wagon and the passengers on the other, with but one cotton umbrella over them, Mr. Bradway and his strange load left the house in search of the husband's place.

The northeast wind was still blowing and the rain still falling. The poor woman, protecting her children as much as she could, was getting wet not only by the rain, but that part which should have been her children's share, soaked still more her already drenched garments by running over the umbrella. But what of the rain! They were soon to be in their new home.

Thus the strange load proceeded on its way through the darkness. The driver had taken a lantern which made the night appear the darker, but a sudden jolt of the wagon put it out. Under the trees, the wind and rain were not driving so badly as on that exposed platform, and around the Bradway place. The road now could not be seen, for it was at that time only a woodman's way, save that part of it which formed the century-old road from Willow Grove to Millville. It was dotted here and there with stumps of trees which now and then threatened to overthrow the wagon and its rain-soaked contents and occupants into the ruts, or the briars, or the sucker-fringed remnants of oaks and pines.

Four mounds, or "hills," as they are called in these regions of flat expanses and sand barrens, had to be gone over and descended. Those rather steep, though diminutive hills, at the time proved quite a strain for the horse and the occupants of the rough conveyance. The road makers since those early days have scraped them flat as the rest of Southern Jersey.

At last, a small hut-like house was reached, the inmates awakened and questioned. Ah! how sweet the sound of the familiar jargon seemed to those starving, half frozen unfortunates. Who could express the feelings of that woman when she, for the first time since she had left the big steamer and Castle Garden, understood what others said? But this was not the place!

However, though it was now about midnight, and in spite of their benumbed fingers, their chilled bodies, and an almost overcoming faintness, brought about by a long fast and exposure, they grew more and more certain that the end of their dreadful experience was near. Gladness born of intense expectation warmed up their hearts, renewed their courage, and also calmed their impatience. A few minutes more and they surely would meet their long absent, long missed, and long desired husband and father.

Presently: "Is this Mr. Kleinfeld's place?" spoke Mr. Bradway, rapping loudly upon the door of the second house they came to, and breaking again the stillness of the night.

"Ya! Ya!" was the response soon coming from a long-whiskered and long-haired head stuck out of a window hastily raised.

A confusion of guttural sounds and strange words drowned the voice of Mr. Bradway crying out: "Somebody's here for you," and in another moment the family of five were hugging and crying and kissing each other. Tears of joy were flowing freely, and sobs of gladness intermingled with noisy exclamations seemed to come from a crowd ten times larger.

Mr. Bradway saw he was no longer needed. He climbed into his wagon, unnoticed during the confusion of that gladsome meeting, and went back on the way to his home, happy to have been instrumental in re-uniting those unfortunate victims of barbaric and sanguinary Russians, in the very last hour of the old year, and the wee first one of the new, which would truly begin for them a new existence in a new world. And his heart was really full of the spirit of those words of the season just ended, "Peace over the earth, and good will among all men."

L. Mounier, 1913

Read at the Vineland Historical Society,
March 8, 1933

Emily Montgomery, who wrote the introduction to this anecdote and laid out the text on the page, is a Senior Communication Studies student at Stockton University. She also has a double minor in Journalism and Spanish and is set to graduate in spring 2021. With experience in the journalism and radio industries and a wide range of interests, she hopes to one day land a job where she can write and communicate on various different platforms.

Sea Breeze, New Jersey:
A Landscape History

Samuel Avery-Quinn

In 1983, *South Jersey Magazine* published a two-part article on the Warner House, a late nineteenth-century resort hotel that once stood in the Cumberland County Bayshore community of Sea Breeze. Shirley Bailey, the magazine's editor, had spent years studying the community, but historical accounts were few. She confessed that her research "proved to be one of the most elusive in our experience," and asked her readers for information in hopes that "someone could help fill in the missing pieces."[1] As the Delaware Bay erodes more of Sea Breeze every year, and the State of New Jersey and environmentalists see the flood-prone community's future as a nature preserve, this article builds on Bailey's research and fills in some missing pieces by tracing the economic, environmental, and social context of the Warner House and visions for the resort's rebirth through the 1930s.

Back Neck

Sea Breeze is located on the northeast side of the Delaware Bay, 2.5 miles (4.km) southeast of the mouth of the Cohansey River. The community, situated a mere five to seven feet above mean sea level, is sinking, like the rest of South Jersey, due to glacial isostatic adjustment or the slow collapse of lands once pushed upwards by the Laurentide Ice Sheet before it retreated over 9,000 years ago.[2] A thin ribbon of barrier beach and a regularly flooded tidal marsh, dominated by smooth cord grass (*Spartina alterniflora)*, surround Sea Breeze.[3] To the northeast, elevation increases, and the marsh becomes swaths of salt hay grass (*Spartina patens*) and spike grass (*Distichlis spicata*), broken by crooked creeks and narrow "guts." Further north, common reed (*Phragmites australis*) and stands of eastern red cedar (*Juniperus virginiana*) give way to farmland and forests of oak (*Quercus*) and pine (*Pinus*) on an upland area called "Back Neck" (Fig. 1). On Back Neck, the elevation

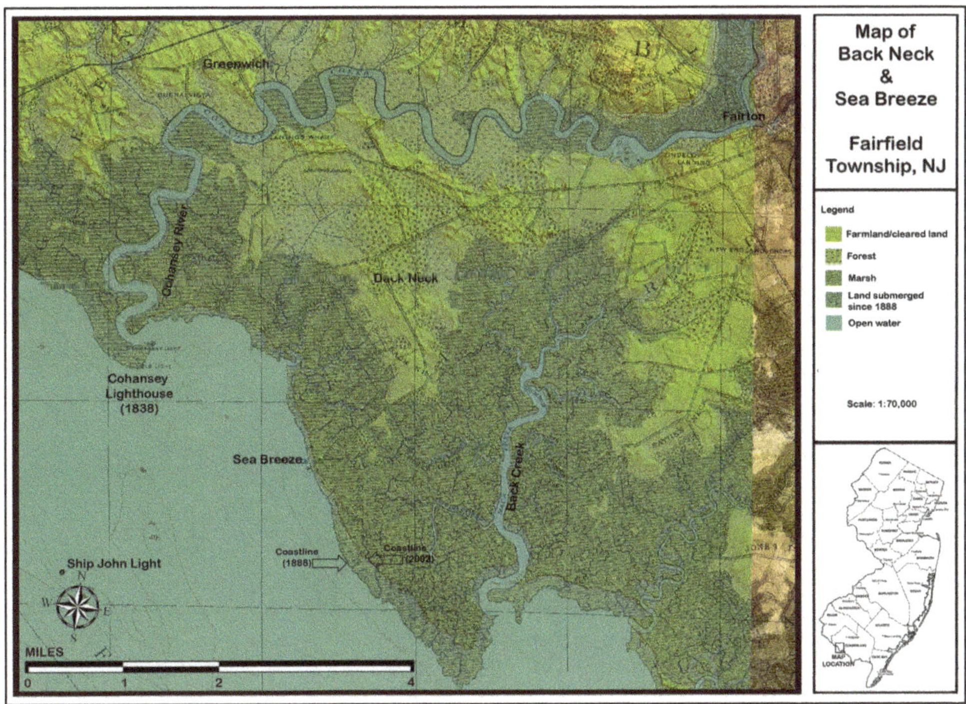

Figure 1. Map of Back Neck and Sea Breeze showing 1888 landscape overlain and georeferenced to align with 2002 topography.[1b]

increases to twelve feet above mean sea level before declining again along the Cohansey River to the north and west and Back Creek to the southeast.

Back Neck was at the periphery of early seventeenth-century European ventures along the Delaware estuary. Dutch trading forts and the colony of New Sweden were well to the west and northwest, leaving the area, like much of South Jersey, as Lenape country.[4] One of the earliest maps depicting the locations of Lenape settlements indicates villages of "Kahansick Indians" along the Cohansey from Back Neck northwards (Fig. 2).[5] By the 1660s, as the Lenape population declined due to disease, displacement, and migration, England imposed a new colonial geography on New Jersey. By 1676, a board of proprietors divided West New Jersey into one hundred shares, granting the ten southernmost shares to John Fenwick.[6] Fenwick's "Salem Tenth" extended from Oldman's Creek to Back Creek. By 1694, London merchant John Bellers held 3,700 acres east of Back Creek, and brewer Joseph Hebley's land covered much of Back Neck and the Sea Breeze marsh.[7] In 1701, Benjamin Davis bought hundreds of acres below Bellars' tract.[8] Although Davis relocated his family in 1726 to Deerfield Township, his name remained tied to Ben Davis Point and the beach running northwest through Sea Breeze.

In the eighteenth century, English, Germans, Irish, French Huguenots, and African American arrivals reshaped Bayshore life.[9] Greenwich became an important inland port opposite Back Neck. To the northeast, Fairton boasted of a blacksmith, gristmill, stores, brick houses, a Presbyterian church, and a wharf. Above Fairton, two mixed-race families, the Goulds and the Pierces, formed the black settlement of Gouldtown. African Americans worked throughout the township, including on Back Neck farms, reached by a road that ran southwest from Fairton past lands that the Barnes, Mulford, Seeley, Sheppard, Wescott, and Whitecar families owned.

In 1819, Ephraim Mulford moved to Back Neck from Roadstown.[10] On Back Neck his field crops included corn, oats, and wheat. He also raised cattle, pigs, and sheep. Farming proved profitable enough that by the 1830s, he began acquiring neighboring farms and built a large brick house for his wife Ruth Wheaton and their children Isaac, Ananias, William, and David. Through the 1840s, Mulford purchased multiple tracts of saltmarsh between Back Creek and the Cohansey River, including most of the marsh south and southwest of Back Neck.[11] High marsh salt hay meadows provided Bayshore farmers like Mulford with pasturage for livestock and salt hay for harvest. The latter was Mulford's most productive crop as salt hay was valuable for feed, stable bedding, and packing material for South Jersey glass manufacturers.[12] When Mulford died in 1868, he left his land holdings to his sons in his last will and testament.

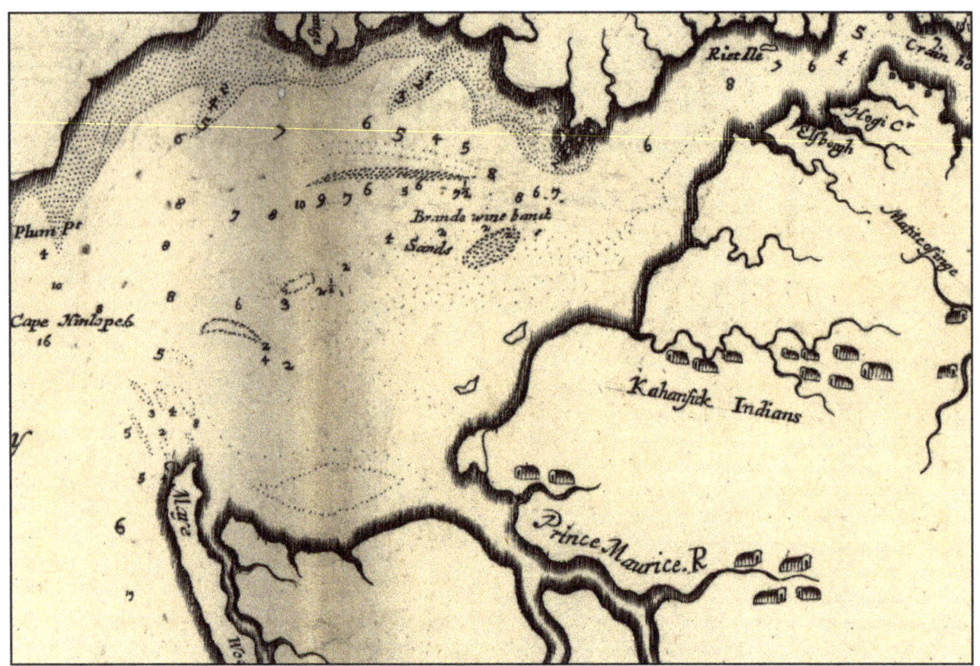

Figure 2. Detail showing the Cohansey River area from Augustine Herrman's (1673) "Virginia and Maryland as it is planted and inhabited this present year." *Source: Augustine Herrman, 1671, Or, Henry Faithorne and Thomas Withinbrook, Virginia and Maryland as it is planted and inhabited this present year* (London: Augustine Herrman and Thomas Withinbrook, 1673). No scale. Courtesy of Library of Congress.

The Warner House

In July 1877, representatives of the Delaware River Steamboat and Transportation Company (DRS&TC) approached David and Isaac Mulford about buying a bayside portion of their farm. The Mulford brothers and the company agreed to a price of $1500 for 120 acres of marsh and upland.[13] The DRS&TC, founded by Capt. Jonathan Cone and a cadre of investors in May 1876, wanted to expand its summer excursion business, and the beach below Back Neck appeared to be a good location for an excursion resort.

Born in Hamdem, Connecticut, to a seafaring family, Cone arrived in Bristol, Pennsylvania, in 1852 and entered the steamboat business on the Upper Delaware River with the wood-hulled steamer SUN.[14] In 1854, Cone and his investors turned to the Harlan & Hollingsworth shipyard in Wilmington, Delaware, to build the line's first iron-hulled steamboat—the THOMAS A. MORGAN.[15] Cone ran the MORGAN on the Upper Delaware River in tandem with the SUN. At the end of April 1857, the Pennsylvania General Assembly approved an act to incorporate the Delaware River Steamboat Company (DRSC) for Cone and his business associates.[16] The company became the preeminent steamboat line on the river above Philadelphia.[17]

In a second contract for the shipyard, Cone wanted a larger and more luxurious boat than the MORGAN. When launched in 1857, the JOHN A. WARNER, named for one of the DRSC's chief investors, a tobacconist from Beverly, New Jersey, was a 527-ton, 220-foot-long, iron-hulled, sidewheel steamboat that could carry 1,200 passengers on three decks (Fig. 3).[18] The WARNER operated on the Upper Delaware with the other two steamers, but by July 1859, the DRSC began special excursion runs to Cape May and the fishing banks near Maurice River Cove using the new vessel.[19]

In May 1862, the DRSC chartered the JOHN A. WARNER to the federal government for the war effort. The WARNER served as a United States Mail Steamer and carried supplies and troops to the Chesapeake Bay and Fortress Monroe in Virginia.[20] Cone remained in command of the vessel, which steamed through the waters of Maryland and Virginia while in service to the Union. Cone and the WARNER returned to the Delaware and began regular scheduled service on June 10, 1865, and increasingly popular summer excursions to riverside resorts and Cape May.[21]

Riverside towns with bathing beaches, picnic groves, or restaurants serving the regional delicacy of planked shad were long popular with excursionists.[22] Steamboats carried Philadelphians upriver to parks at Andalusia and Torresdale and downriver to Penns Grove, Silver Grove (Pennsville), Cape May, as well as Augustine and Collins Beaches in Delaware. In the 1810s, when proprietors first opened vacation hotels at Cape Island, later Cape May City, they created a resort

Figure 3. The JOHN A. WARNER at Riverton, New Jersey (1899). Courtesy of the Independence Seaport Museum, Philadelphia, PA.

that would compete with Long Branch, New Jersey, and Newport, Rhode Island, for genteel vacationers.[23] The resort, however, was remote and overland travel proved difficult. Schooners and steamboats provided preferred routes from Philadelphia and ports in Delaware and Maryland. Cape May travel was profitable for steamboat lines, but would, like Cape May's fortunes, face challenges.

On July 1, 1854, when the first train of the Camden and Atlantic Railroad arrived at Atlantic City, Cape May proprietors feared they would lose vacationers to the new resort.[24] Six years of competition later, the Civil War further shook Cape May's economy and cut off regular clientele from the South. In 1860, Cape May boosters found hope in what became the West Jersey Railroad, linking Camden and Woodbury to Glassboro, Bridgeton, and Millville, and, by 1863, Cape Island.[25] Although the line helped offset the loss of vacationers from the South, with only a four-hour trip from Philadelphia, many of the new vacationers were day-trippers. In 1868, the railroad company built the Sea Breeze Excursion House at Cape May (Fig. 4).[26] The Sea Breeze boasted verandahs, a ballroom, bar, billiard rooms, dining rooms, and bathhouses, but had few private rooms and the amenities primarily catered to day-trippers. The success of the Sea Breeze and waves of new excursionists spurred growth at the resort that continued until the Panic of 1873, a time of severe national economic downturn.

For steamboat companies running to Cape May, day-trippers became an important part of their summer revenue. Steamboat companies had a problem, however, as their boats traveled at a slower pace than the railroad. Although steamboat companies offered reduced fares, onboard meals, and entertainment, their excursionists arrived at Cape Island with only a few hours to spare at the resort if they were to return to Philadelphia by evening. By 1876, the DRSC sought a location that would allow excursionists more time for leisure.

As the WARNER ran to Cape May and the DRSC considered alternative sites closer to Philadelphia, Cone and his associates formed the Delaware River Steamboat & Transportation Company (DRS&TC). The new company reflected Cone's growing interest in the summer excursion market on the lower stretches of the estuary.[27] For the first year of the DRS&TC's operations, the new company relied on the JOHN A. WARNER—a boat still registered to the DRSC. While the WARNER steamed down the estuary for Cape May and other points on the bay, the DRSC continued to operate the TWILIGHT and the COLUMBIA from Philadelphia's Chestnut Street Wharf for runs to riverfront communities upriver.[28]

In the summer of 1876, the DRS&TC settled on Fortescue as a promising location for excursion runs. The village was 25 miles closer to Philadelphia than Cape Island, had a small hotel, and a broad beach.[29] Bringing excursionists to Fortescue was, however, not without difficulties. When the WARNER arrived, the steamboat had to drop anchor and disembark passengers one skiff-load at a time.[30] Although Fortescue offered good crabbing and fishing, there were few amenities and many mosquitoes. If the DRS&TC was to have a profitable Bayshore venture, the company needed a location even closer to Philadelphia.

Figure 4. Woodcut depicting the Sea Breeze Excursion House, Cape Island. From *The Ocean Resort: Life at Cape May* (Philadelphia: Allen, Lane, and Scott, 1876), 22.

The Mulfords' salt marsh was only 35 miles from Philadelphia, had a broad beach, and enough elevated land for resort buildings. The 120-acre tract the DRS&TC purchased, however, lacked infrastructure and the only access from Back Neck was a causeway in poor condition.[31] By March, construction of the resort began. The DRS&TC hired George Lloyd, an African American resident of Back Neck, to help

Figure 5. The Warner House, front view. Courtesy of the Lummis Library, Cumberland County Historical Society, Greenwich, New Jersey.

raise the roadbed through the marsh and cart sand to level the hotel site.[32] The company also hired D. Edward Smith and Albert Conover, owners of a mill and lumber yard in Bridgeton, to build the hotel and outbuildings.[33] Construction of the hotel was rapid—with foundations laid by late March, the building's wood frame erected in April, enclosed and plastered, and, by late May, the hotel was ready for painting by Charles Scrull of Bridgeton.[34] In June, the company advertised the resort as "Sea Breeze" and the hotel as the "Warner House."

The Warner House shared a style common among Cape May hotels (Fig. 5).[35] The two-story, 200 x 35-foot hotel had first- and second-story verandahs wrapped around the building with wooden cross members forming balustrades or railings. A square cupola topped the low-pitched roof. Inside, the building was an excursion house in the model of the Sea Breeze at Cape Island. On the upper floor, forty guest rooms lined a hallway.[36] Downstairs, the two largest rooms were a 113 x 17-foot dining room and a 93 x 16-foot excursion room featuring an organ. Between the rooms, the hotel's front door opened onto a parlor, a bar, a reading room, and a billiard room. The hotel's water supply came from two 1,200-gallon capacity water tanks. In 1878, when David Scattergood published a guide to the Delaware River, he included Sea Breeze as a destination for excursionists and printed a woodcut view from the northwest depicting the resort with gardens beside the hotel and bathhouses along the beach (Fig. 6).[37] Nearby, builders erected a barn, a two-story 'ten-pin' bowling alley, and, 546 feet from the hotel, a steamboat pier.

When the Warner House opened on June 18, 1877, Arnold Shailer was the hotel's first proprietor. Each day of the summer season, the JOHN A. WARNER, with a "FOR SEA BREEZE" pennant fluttering from its foremast, arrived with excursionists to fanfare and a tolling bell.[38] Other excursionists arrived with less ceremony, either conveyed by a stage line from Fairton or cruising down the Cohansey from Bridgeton aboard steamboats such as the CITY OF BRIDGETON or the CHAMPION.

Figure 6. Woodcut view of the Warner House with some embellishments including the exaggerated height of the hotel and cupola, the flat roof with broad cornice pieces, and pier much closer to the hotel than as described in accounts of the grounds. From David Scattergood, *The Delaware River Illustrated from Philadelphia to the Sea* (Philadelphia: David Scattergood, 1878), 16.

Visitors could stay in the Warner House's guest rooms with window screens to keep out biting greenhead flies and mosquitoes for $2 a day or $10 a week. However, far more excursionists, having paid the DRS&TC's fare of 60 cents, were day-trippers.[39] In 1878, Shailer contracted a yacht, the Cornelia, for fishing on the bay.[40] He also hired string bands, orchestras, and theater troupes to entertain guests. Lunch in the hotel dining room of oysters, clams, diamondback terrapins, and fish was a staple when visiting the resort.

On Sea Breeze's first Fourth of July weekend, the Warner and the City of Bridgeton arrived, their decks teeming with excursionists.[41] Two dozen craft anchored offshore for the weekend's yacht races. The hotel staff was hard-pressed to keep up with the demand for beer and ice cream. With thousands of excursionists crowding the beach, the Fourth of July became the resort's most popular weekend every year. Other popular weekends included "Salt Water Day," with events for local farmers, and, throughout the season, discounted oyster dinners and clambakes for excursionists booking passage on the Warner.[42] That first summer's daily routines and special events would continue at the resort for the next twelve years.

Natural, legal, and economic challenges would, however, reshape the resort's summertime rhythms. On October 23, 1878, the remnants of a hurricane brought a 10-foot storm surge, high winds, and heavy rain to the Bayshore.[43] The storm damaged or destroyed almost every building in Fortescue, tore the roof off the Presbyterian church in Fairton, wrecked a ship at the mouth of the Cohansey, and battered the Cohansey Lighthouse, causing irreparable damage.[44] At Sea Breeze, the tide flowed across the grounds, carrying away bathhouses, tearing the barn from its foundations, and damaging the hotel. When the waters receded, the DRS&TC hired Smith and Conover to begin repairs.[45] By June 1879, the DRS&TC boasted that the John A. Warner and Sea Breeze had been "refitted" for the season.[46] Despite that cheery perspective, Sea Breeze faced a costly period of storms, some the remnants of hurricanes, that lasted through 1904.

In 1885, the DRSC reorganized as the Upper Delaware River Transportation Company (UDRTC) and relocated the company's office from Bristol, Pennsylvania, to Beverly, New Jersey.[47] The DRS&TC had not filed either annual reports or paid taxes to the State of Pennsylvania since 1879. In 1883, Pennsylvania Governor Robert E. Pattison, declared the charter for the DRS&TC "... forfeited and their chartered privileges at an end."[48] Despite the moribund condition of the DRS&TC as a public entity, the company drafted a deed in 1886 and transferred Sea Breeze to the new UDRTC.

For the WARNER's runs to Sea Breeze, the reorganized company reduced excursion fares to 50 cents. They also hired Thomas Howard, a saloonkeeper from Philadelphia, as the hotel's new proprietor. Local authorities soon stripped the Warner House of its liquor license, however, and, not long after, arrested Howard on charges of selling beer without a license.[49] The company scrambled, hired George Bates as proprietor, and ran more advertisements emphasizing Sea Breeze as an ideal destination for families, church groups, and Sunday schools.[50] Notices in area newspapers of church and Sunday school outings to Sea Breeze increased, including excursions by black churches from Bridgeton, Chester, and Philadelphia.[51]

By 1888, the WARNER's summer runs included stops at Chester, Silver Grove (forerunner of Riverview Beach in Pennsville), and Sea Breeze.[52] Sea Breeze remained profitable enough that by the summer of 1889, the UDRTC extended the pier, repaired the boardwalk, and built a dance pavilion. Plans for a new switchback railway ride would wait until the next season—a season that would not come.[53]

A Landscape of Ruins

On April 15, 1890, a Bridgeton reporter found George Lloyd staring at the smoldering remains of the Warner House.[54] Early that morning, a fire reduced the excursion hotel to a mound of blackened lumber and ashes (Fig. 7). In the *Evening News*, George Nixon estimated that losses were as much as $20,000.[55] When directors of the UDRTC toured Sea Breeze, and insurance investigators began to assess the damage, Nixon wondered how long it would be before the resort was rebuilt.

That summer, the Warner House remained a pile of rubble.[56] The bathhouses, dance pavilion, ten-pin alley, and pier were untouched by the fire, leaving the resort's amenities comparable to smaller resorts along the estuary. The WARNER continued runs to Sea Breeze, but the UDRTC added a stop at Augustine Beach. The UDRTC wrote new advertisements tinged with nostalgia and appealed to excursionists' loyalty. "On

WARNER HOUSE DESTROYED

A DISASTEROUS FIRE AT SEA BREEZE.

A Big Fire Destroys the Warner House at Sea Breeze Wednesday Morning.

WEDNESDAY.

A week ago William T. Bowen contracted to do about five hundred dollars worth of work at Sea Breeze and this morning he started for the popular Bay resort to commence the work. Just as he reached Fairton he met Proprietor George Bates and Constable R. F. Ayars driving to Bridgeton, and Mr. Bates asked the question:

"Where are you going, Mr. Bowen?"

"To Sea Breeze," replied the popular painter.

"I wouldn't go if I were you," said Mr. Bates.

"Well, I'm going any way," answered Mr. Bowen.

"Well," said Mr. Bates," If you do there won't be anything to do, for the Warner House was burned to the ground this morning."

Mr. Bowen wheeled his horse around and came directly to Bridgeton, bringing with him the news, and a half an hour after his arrival nothing else was heard on the street but the burning of the Warner House.

A PIONEER reporter hurriedly found Constable Ayars to learn from him the details of the disaster, Mr. Bates having gone to Philadelphia immediately upon the 8.05 train.

Mr. Ayars and Mr. Bates went to Sea Breeze yesterday afternoon to make arrangements for the season, and late at night retired as usual, Mr. Ayars going to room No. 20. About fifteen minutes of two o'clock, this morning, Mrs. George Lloyd, wife of the gentleman who has been keeping the house during the summer, was awakened by the crying of her infant child, and thought she smelled smoke. Hurriedly running down the back stairway, she discovered the lower part of the house in flames. In an instant, she rushed up stairs to alarm the household. Mr. Bates was awakened, and he in turn waked Mr. Ayars.

By this time the flames were carrying everything before them, and the hastily awakened members of the household had barely time to escape with their lives. Mr. Ayars lost his watch, a buffalo robe, rubber coat and whip. One of the carpenters who has been at work upon the toboggan slide lost his hat, two suits of clothes and his boots. The family of Mr. Lloyd saved but little, one of the children being left entirely without any clothes, Mrs. Lloyd carried out two blankets with which she wrapped up her children, and beyond these, not a single article was saved from the house.

When the occupants of the house got out of the burning hotel they found that every part of the building was in flames. The wind blew from the north east, and the thatch covering of the board walk took fire and in a few moments the walk was burned to the waters edge. The pier was saved by cutting off the board walk from it.

How the fire started is a mystery. Mr. Bates and Mr. Ayars, after careful examination are inclined to think it is the work of an incendiary. The fire started either in or under the dining room. There was no fire in the dining room, and the only fire in the house was in the kitchen range, and it is not believed that the fire originated from that. One of the carpenters who has been working upon the toboggan slide said that when he got down stairs there was more fire underneath than over the dining room floor.

The bowling alley, toboggan slide, and stables were not burned.

The Warner House was the property of the Upper Delaware River Transportation Company, of Philadelphia, and was leased by Mr. Bates. All the furnishings of the house belonged to the company named. The building was erected in 1877, by Smith & Conover of this city, and one of that firm said this morning that the building with all its furnishings were worth from $15,000 to $20,000.

Whether the place will be rebuilt is unknown. The probabilities are that it will, as it is one of the best paying resorts on the Bayshore. If work was pushed rapidly, a new building could be erected by the time the full season was open. The reporter could not learn this morning whether or not there was any insurance upon the building.

Figure 7. Account of the April 15, 1890, fire that destroyed the Warner House. From "Warner House Destroyed," *Bridgeton Pioneer*, April 17, 1890.

SUNDAY, June 29, the favorite Steamer John A. Warner will resume daily trips to Sea Breeze and Augustine Pier, the popular resorts for families and children," claimed one advertisement.[57] Another ad reassured excursionists that at Sea Breeze, "there's a fine time for everybody. Music, dancing, bathing, fishing and boating are among the leading features of this agreeable day's outing."[58] In 1891, however, the company reassigned the Warner to summer runs upriver from Philadelphia, while the Columbia ran to other downriver resorts.[59] With the UDRTC no long servicing Sea Breeze, the last steamboat run to the resort may have been an August 1891 excursion of the Freundschaft Sängerbund, a German club from Philadelphia who arrived aboard the Edwin Forrest.[60]

For fourteen years, to the consternation of local residents, the UDRTC would neither rebuild nor sell their Sea Breeze property. On December 10, 1891, the *Bridgeton Pioneer* claimed that "a Cumberland County gentleman of means . . . has gone so far as to acquaint the company that owns the place, that he desires to purchase [it]," but that the directors, while not unanimous in their response, refused to sell.[61] The company to which that gentleman appealed was no longer the Jonathan Cone-dominated firm that established Sea Breeze. Even before Cone's death in 1887, the UDRTC was pulling back from its earlier ventures, concentrating on travel closer to Philadelphia.[62] When Cone died, the company's interest in having a stake in the Bayshore's resort market ended with him. Leasing rights to the salt hay meadows at Sea Breeze may have provided enough income that the directors retained the property while trying to agree on what more to do with it. Changes to excursion travel on the Delaware also helped defer a final decision.

In the 1890s, amusement parks became the most popular resorts along the estuary, tapping Americans' fascination with novelty and mechanization. In 1890, Lincoln Park opened near Paulsboro, New Jersey, offering a beer garden, large music shell, a merry-go-round, toboggan slide, and concession stands around a three-story hotel.[63] In 1895, William "Billy" Thompson opened a 600-acre tract near Westville, New Jersey, as "Washington Park On the Delaware," teeming with rides, orchestra stages, Vaudeville shows, and a sea of concession stands.[64] Thompson's venture, like Lincoln Park, and, further south, Germania Park and Riverview Beach, depended on ferries and steamboats for patrons. For the UDRTC, facing a dwindling pool of passengers and competition from shore resorts, servicing amusement parks provided more stable revenue than running a Bayshore resort. By the late 1890s, however, interest in some riverside amusement parks began to wane. In 1896, Germania Park declared bankruptcy, and a year later, Lincoln Park was on the auction block.[65] Although on the Upper Delaware, the newer Burlington Island Park, and on the Lower Delaware, Washington Park and Riverview Beach, continued to draw crowds beyond the 1890s economic slump in the estuary's amusement park industry, contracts for bringing excursionists to these amusement parks were competitive. Soon after 1900, Billy Thompson ran his own line of steamers from Camden and Philadelphia to Washington Park while steamboats of the Wilmington-based Wilson Line crowded the pier at Riverview Beach.

Through the 1890s, Sea Breeze became a landscape of memories tended by George Lloyd, who lived with his family on the second floor of the bowling alley.[66] In July 1893, the *Evening News* reported that "Sea Breeze catches a good many Bridgeton people, and also persons from the surrounding country . . . Nearly every day some picnic party goes to visit this old favorite place for a day's pleasure."[67] Fishing trips, picnics, and church outings remained regular features of Sea Breeze. On August 8, 1900, the paper observed that "Sea Breeze is getting to be quite a resort. Over a hundred spent the day there Thursday."[68] As locals visited Sea Breeze, they told stories of the resort's renewal.

In June 1890, the *Evening News* reported a rumor that the UDRTC bought the buildings of Ridgway Park near Philadelphia and would move them to Sea Breeze.[69] According to another tale, Billy Thompson purchased the resort.[70] In September 1899, an excursionist returned from a picnic at Sea Breeze and wrote a letter to the *Evening News*. "We think that if some of our moneyed men were to interest themselves in Sea Breeze . . . they would find a safe investment," the letter claimed, and then decried that, "it seems to be too bad for a place . . . to lay in a pile of ruins and to be carted off by every Tom, Dick, and Harry."[71]

Visions of Sea Breeze's renewal would remain on hold for years. In 1900, the UDRTC reorganized as the Delaware River Navigation Company (DRNC) and expanded its routes to ports in Delaware, cutting into the territory of the Wilson Line of steamboats.[72] The Wilson Line also expanded its runs to the Upper Delaware River above Philadelphia. The ensuing "steamboat war" eroded both companies' profits. In 1905, the directors of the DRNC sold Sea Breeze for $2,000 to Clara Wagner, a widow from Philadelphia.[73] Wagner may have purchased the property as an investment, expecting income from leasing the salt hay meadows as she did little else with the property. During her ownership, buildings fell further into disrepair, and the pier collapsed. Before he died in 1915, George Lloyd moved his family to Back Neck, where he and his sons worked for the Mulfords and managed a small orchard.[74] Outings to Sea Breeze continued, but with less mention in local papers than before Wagner's purchase.[75]

BETTER THAN VENICE

On March 17, 1918, a classified ad ran in the *Philadelphia Inquirer*. "FOR SALE CHEAP—120 acres of land, on Delaware River known as Sea Breeze, near Bridgeton, lots of salt hay on this property. Write or call owner."[76] Sea Breeze did not stay on the market for long. By April 3, 1918, Wagner transferred the property for $1 to Joseph Wise of the Chicago-based American Investment Association (AIA).[77] Wise soon hired a surveyor, Furman Sheppard, of Cedarville, to survey and divide the property into dozens of small lots.[78] Wise held the property title, but promised Wagner the revenue from Sea Breeze without her needing to sign the deeds every time he sold a lot. For this convenience, Wise and his partner, Frank Zini, took hefty commissions.

Wise advertised the property as "Sea Breeze, Subdivision on the Delaware Bay." J. Ward Richardson, the editor of the *Bridgeton Evening News*, praised Wise's plan, claiming that "it is very likely that Sea Breeze will this season become again a mecca for pleasure seekers."[79] Buyers would join the Sea Breeze Outing Club, with free use of a new hotel, bathhouses, and amusements. In their grandest vision, the AIA would rebuild the pier and have the Wilson Line run steamboat excursions, just like the "CHARLES A. WARNER" [sic] years before. Wise ran advertisements in area papers and distributed handbills on the streets of Philadelphia (Fig. 8). Sea Breeze was a fabulous investment opportunity—like Venice, Italy, before it became a great city but with a "many times betters start." All the resort needed would be people buying lots "as low as $100 each."[80] Wise urged his readers to invest before it was too late as choice lots were already going for $500 each. He also pointed to his company's success "out west" at Lakewood Terrace and White Lake Highlands.

Figure 8. American Investment Association advertisement for "Sea Breeze, a Subdivision on the Delaware Bay." From "Sea Breeze, Subdivision on the Delaware Bay," *Bridgeton Evening News*, May 4, 1918.

AMERICAN INVESTMENT ASSOCIATION

With an Authorized Capital of $100,000 to Promote

SEA BREEZE

Subdivision on Delaware Bay

The Sea Breeze

that the "Charles A. Warner," excursion steamer of Philadelphia, used to make daily trips to—that used to be visited by thousands of people for miles around—that used to be the playground of the older folks—that's the place we have reference to, and we are calling your attention to it because it is going to be "brought back into its own" by the

Sea Breeze Outing Club

Not as a private-owned place controlled by a few and profitable to a few, but as a semi-public place where all will have a chance to take an interest and share its benefits—

Listen: We have proven repeatedly, and it is reasonable to understand that Realty values of any kind are brought about by human activity, human presence—for example:

Years ago a few thousand human beings were driven from their soil into the sea. In spite of the great difficulties and absolute unadaptability for what it developed into the fact that people were there made this part of the sea grow into a little town, which afterwards developed into one of the world's most famous, most beautiful, and most admired cities. This place is known as Venice, in Italy. Now there is no anology of this to Sea Breeze. We have no such colossal hopes; besides Sea Breeze has a many times better start than Venice had. Sea Breeze has ample and many unequalled facilities as a playground.—The long, shallow beach, the beautiful white sand, ideal for bathing and boating, the adjacent fishing, crabbing, gunning, etc., finest on the coast—everything to develop it into one of Jersey's leading resorts. All it lacked was the boost behind and an interest in it by a sufficient number of people. A sufficient number of people can extraordinarily enhance land values anywhere, and they do, but with few exceptions the majority rarely benefit by it. This is going to be one of the exceptions. We have furnished the boost and

We Guarantee to Get 1000 People Financially Interested in Sea Breeze

And this guarantees the success of Sea Breeze. It is the duty of people of Cumberland and adjoining counties to buy lots now and aid in the developing of Sea Breeze, because you will be the one to enjoy it most; but we don't ask you to buy as a duty, but buy now; make your reservation immediately, or later you will belong to that crowd which will be saying: "Why only a short time ago I had an opportunity to buy lots at Sea Breeze as low as $100 each."

Let us tell you about our properties at White Lake Highlands and Lakewood Terrace: Less than 5 years ago, Lakewood was woodland. In one year it had over 5000 owners; and in a few years it developed a R. R. station, street car line, hundreds of bungalows, movies, stores, club house, churches, etc. And now has over 35,000 visitors annually. To whom does the credit belong? Well really, we'll admit, the people did it all after they were started. What was done at Lakewood can be done at Sea Breeze, on a proportionally smaller scale, but just as effective for those who get in on the ground floor.

Watch the newspapers and theatres for our advertising offers but make your first reservation NOW!

The Choicest Lots

NOW for ONLY $500

The Finest Beach on the Whole Jersey Coast

For Particulars Write

AMERICAN INVESTMENT ASSOCIATION

Suite 20-21-22 Baxter Building 1414 S. Penn Square Opp. South Side City Hall **PHILADELPHIA, PA.**

Before too many people could buy Sea Breeze lots, Philadelphia police arrested Wise and Zini on a warrant issued by the Cook County, Illinois, District Attorney's office. On June 18, 1918, Chicago authorities, alleging that the AIA ran a fraudulent lottery scheme offering land at a Michigan "resort," raided the company's office, arrested the office manager, and seized records.[81] In Chicago, Wise had hired agents to canvas movie theaters, wait in the lobby, hand out lottery tickets, and collect contact information. Unbeknownst to the movie-goers, everyone was a winner—so long as they paid the AIA as much as $18 for a one-eighth-acre lot.[82] Wise kept little track of lot sales, and anyone visiting northern Muskegon County would have been hard-pressed to determine which small slice of forest was their prize.[83]

When police arrested Wise, *The Philadelphia Inquirer* labeled him a "shore realty dealer" and an "alleged land shark."[84] *The North American* claimed that Wise swindled hundreds of Philadelphians for Sea Breeze land "guaranteed to be high and dry."[85] The article quoted the Cumberland County Clerk suggesting otherwise: "The place was once a summer resort, but today it is wet and swamp." However, the Philadelphia District Attorney did not file charges over Wise and Zini's Sea Breeze dealings, and the court released

Figure 9. Sea Breeze in 1941. (Top) Sea Breeze shorefront with Jesse Smith's Seabreeze Hotel on right. (Bottom) Sketch of Seabreeze Hotel. Mixed-media sketches based on photo in Henry C. Beck, "River of Industry: 'Bellboy' of Old Warner House Is Still Down at Sea Breeze," *Courier-Post* (Camden, NJ), June 16, 1941.

the men on bail with orders to present themselves to Chicago authorities. After his arraignment, Wise failed to pay taxes on Sea Breeze. By August 1919, Fairfield Township announced a tax sale.[86] Neither Wise nor any of the 28 Philadelphia residents holding Sea Breeze deeds contested the sale. The Township sold Sea Breeze for $39.75 to Albert W. Kauffmann, a lawyer and realty speculator from Bridgeton.[87] Kauffmann held the property until 1923 when he transferred Sea Breeze to William Cauthorn of Greenwich.[88]

Cauthorn ran Greenwich's general store and planned to revive the resort.[89] By 1927, he let several local men use the marsh for the Sea Breeze Rod and Gun Club.[90] Cauthorn also let Jesse E. Smith, a muskrat trapper, build a new hotel on the site of the Warner House.[91] Smith's Seabreeze Hotel was a four-bay, rectangular, two-story, wood-frame building covered in plain wood siding and fronted by a screened first-floor porch. The structure lacked the architectural pretensions of the Warner House (Fig. 9). The hotel remained unfinished for years. In August 1930, a reporter traveling to Fairton noted that "one must pass by the road that wanders down to Sea Breeze, a tiny bay resort with a hotel, which built on the site of one that burned years ago, has not been occupied since its completion. . . . But several small cabins are underway fringing the Bayshore."[92] The Seabreeze stood, if not functioned, until burning down in 1942. Although Smith lost his hotel as well as his stockpile of muskrat pelts, those cabins were the first of 17 lots Cauthorn sold between 1927 and 1940.[93] The sales established Sea Breeze as a community of summer homes and year-round residences.

In 2010, the State of New Jersey bought and subsequently demolished 26 homes in Sea Breeze.[94] The move to demolish the southern half of Sea Breeze occurred three years after the state and Fairfield Township paid for a revetment to protect the community from erosion, but within months the bay reduced the barrier to a disjointed sheet of concrete rubble.[95] The Sea Breeze buyouts were part of an evolving coastal hazard mitigation strategy that had long shifted away from efforts to harden shorelines with groins, jetties, and sea walls to a soft strategy that favored expensive beach replenishment efforts at Jersey Shore resorts and efforts to restore Bayshore salt marshes. In 1995, the state had launched, with limited funding, the Blue Acres program to buy and demolish neighborhoods in flood-prone coastal communities. Although the aftermath of Superstorm Sandy in 2012 would pump hundreds of millions of dollars into the Blue Acres program, in 2010, the state relied on a patchwork of state and federal funding for coastal buyouts such as at Sea Breeze.[96] While environmentalists and planners hail buyouts as a model response to climate change, at Sea Breeze, displacement and loss seem inevitable, and the bay may soon scour from the landscape all evidence of what was once a popular resort.[97]

About the Author

Samuel Avery-Quinn is a University College Senior Lecturer at Appalachian State University in Boone, North Carolina. He is the author of *Cities of Zion: The Holiness Movement and Methodist Camp Meeting Towns in America* (Lexington Books, 2019) and numerous articles on American religious history, material culture, and landscape. Research for this article was part of a larger study of landscape change in South Jersey during the late 19th and early 20th centuries. A Vineland native, three generations of his family vacationed at Sea Breeze, Fortescue, and Gandy's Beach.

Endnotes

1 Shirley Bailey, "The Warner House at Sea Breeze, Part 1," *South Jersey Magazine* 12, no. 3 (Summer 1983a), 19–24; ______, "The Warner House at Sea Breeze, Part 2," *South Jersey Magazine* 12, no. 4 (Fall 1983b), 30–32.

1b Sources for Figure 1: NJDEP 10-meter Digital Elevation Grid of the Maurice, Salem, and Cohansey Watershed Management Area (WMA 17). NJ Department of Environmental Protection (NJDEP), Office of Information Resources Management (OIRM), Bureau of Geographic Information and Analysis (BGIA). 7.5-minute DEM, 2002 edition. Trenton, NJ: NJDEP. http://www.state.nj.us/dep/gis/digidownload/zips/wmalattice/wma17lat.zip; George Hammell Cook and Cornelius Clarkson Vermeule, *A Topographical Map of the Vicinity of Bridgeton from Alloway, Elmer and Newfield Southward to the Delaware Bay* (New York: Julius Bien & Co., 1888). Map scale =1:70,000. David Rumsey Historical Map Collection, http://www.davidrumsey.com/rumsey/download.pl?image=/D0110/2902016.sid.

2 The massive Laurentide Ice Sheet once covered New England and New York, and its shear weight caused the Earth's crust beneath it to sink in response. In southern New Jersey, land bulged upward. Starting 24,000 years ago, as the ice sheet retreated, land in New England and New York rose while, in South Jersey, land began and continues to sink. See A. R. Simms, L. Lisiecki, G. Gebbie, P. L. Whitehouse, J. F. Clark, "Balancing the Last Glacial Maximum (LGM) Sea-Level Budget," *Quaternary Science Reviews* 205 (2019), 143–53; B. D. DeJong, P. R. Bierman, W. L. Newell, T. M. Rittenour, G. Balco, and D. H. Rood, "Pleistocene Relative Sea Levels

in the Chesapeake Bay Region and Their Implications for the Next Century," *GSA Today* 25, no. 8 (2015), 4–10; Glenn A. Milne, "Glacial Isostatic Adjustment," *Handbook of Sea-Level Research*, eds. Ian Shennan, Antony Long, Benjamin Horton (Hoboken: John Wiley & Sons, 2015), 421–37; Kenneth Miller, Peter Sugarman, James Browning, Benjamin Horton, Alissa Stanley, Alicia Kahn, Jane Putegrove, and Michael Aucott, "Sea-Level Rise in New Jersey Over the Past 5,000 Years: Implications to Anthropogenic Changes," *Global and Planetary Change* 66, no. 1–2 (2009), 10–18.

3 For more information on New Jersey's salt marshes, see Ralph W. Tiner Jr., *Wetlands of New Jersey* (Newton Comer, MA: U.S. Fish and Wildlife Service, National Wetlands Inventory, 1985). For an introduction to the complex ecology of North American salt marshes, see Judith Weis and Carol Butler, *Salt Marshes: A Natural and Unnatural History* (New Brunswick: Rutgers University Press, 2009).

4 For work on the interactions of Dutch, Finns, Swedes, and Lenapes in the Delaware Valley, see Jean Soderlund, *Lenape Country: Delaware Valley Society Before William Penn* (Philadelphia: University of Pennsylvania Press, 2015); Amy Schutt, *Peoples of the River Valleys: The Odyssey of the Delaware Indians* (Philadelphia: University of Pennsylvania Press, 2007).

5 The biodiversity, predictable seasonal peaks in migratory birds and spawning fish, and accessible streams for fish seines or traps in the marshes fringing Back Neck would have provided local Lenapes a stable and substantial food source. However, with no archaeological site reports on Back Neck filed with the New Jersey State Historic Preservation Office, evidence for indigenous uses of the marsh is left to local stories, scattered projectile points, pottery, and possibly a long-ago looted shell midden.

6 See John Pomfret, *The Province of West New Jersey, 1609–1702* (Princeton: Princeton University Press, 1956); Lucius Q. C. Elmer, *History of the Early Settlement and Progress of Cumberland County, New Jersey* (Bridgeton: George F. Nixon, 1869), 5–13.

7 Thomas Cushing and Charles E. Sheppard, *History of the Counties of Gloucester, Salem, and Cumberland New Jersey, with Biographical Sketches of their Prominent Citizens* (Philadelphia: Everts and Peck, 1883), 507–508; Elmer, *History . . . of Cumberland County,* 18–19. See also George Hampton, "Places and Place Names of Cumberland Co.," *Vineland Historical Magazine* 9, No. 1 (January 1924), 156–63.

8 Thomas Shourds, *History and Genealogy of Fenwick's Colony* (Bridgeton, NJ: George F. Nixon, 1876), 530–31.

9 See Sharron Morita, *Bridgeton, New Jersey: City on the Cohansey* (Charleston: The History Press, 2012); Wendel White, Deborah Willis, Stedman Graham, and Clement Alexander Price, *Small Towns, Black Lives: African American Communities in Southern New Jersey* (Oceanville: The Noyes Museum of Art, 2003); Henry Beck, *Forgotten Towns of Southern New Jersey* (New Brunswick: Rutgers University Press, 1983), 191–202; William Steward and Theophilus Steward, *Gouldtown: A Very Remarkable Settlement of Ancient Date* (Philadelphia: J. B. Lippincott, 1913); Cushing and Sheppard, *History of the Counties of Gloucester, Salem, and Cumberland New Jersey,* 582–632, 662–79; Elmer, *History . . . of Cumberland County,* 13–14, 20–21, 38.

10 Cushing and Sheppard, *History of the Counties of Gloucester, Salem, and Cumberland New Jersey,* 678–79.

11 See, for instance, Cumberland County Deed Book 67: 618, and Cumberland County Deed Book 59: 155.

12 In 1850, Mulford had only seventeen head of cattle, but harvested 150 tons of salt hay—1850 U.S. Census, Cumberland County, New Jersey, Fairfield Township, Agricultural Schedule, 217–18, in-house microfilm; New Jersey State Archives, Trenton. For the importance of salt hay for the Bayshore economy, see Janet Foster, "A Water-Based Landscape: Meadow Banks and Salt Marshes," *Down Jersey: From Bayshore to Seashore, a Guidebook for the Annual Conference of the Vernacular Architecture Forum*, ed. Robert Craig (Galloway: Richard Stockton University, 2014), 26–29; Kimberly Sebold, "From Marsh to Farm: The Landscape Transformation of Coastal New Jersey," Historic American Buildings Survey/Historic American Engineering Record. New Jersey Coastal Heritage Trail. National Park Service (Washington, DC: U.S. Department of the Interior, 1992).

13 Cumberland County Deed Book 150: 422; Cumberland County Deed Book 150: 470.

14 For Cone, see: Richard Elliott, *The Saga of the Wilson Line: Last of the Steamboats* (Cambridge: Tidewater Publishers, 1970), 5–6; William Whitney Cone, *Some Account of the Cone Family in America, Principally of the Descendants of Daniel Cone, who settled in Haddam, Connecticut, in 1662* (Topeka: Crane and Co., 1903), 401. Cone served as the Sun's captain while providing twice daily trips starting in May 1852. For Whildin, see "Died," *Public Ledger* (Philadelphia, PA), April 3, 1852, 2. For the Sun's scheduled stops including Beverly, Burlington, Bristol, and touching at Torresdale, Bickley's Landing, and College Wharf on an as needed basis, see "Advertisement," *The Sun* (Philadelphia, PA) May 10, 1852, 4.

15 William M. Lytle and Forrest R. Holdcamper, *Merchant Steam Vessels of the United States, 1790–1868*, revised and edited by C. Bradford Mitchell and Kenneth R. Hall (Staten Island, NY: The Steamship Historical Society of America, Inc., 1975), 211.

16 State of Pennsylvania, *Laws of the General Assembly of the State of Pennsylvania* (Harrisburg, PA: A. Boyd Hamilton, 1857), 364.

17 It appears, however, the Morgan's acquisition caused Cone some financial distress for in August 1855, he

offered a ⅛ share of the new steamer for sale as well as a ¼ interest in the SUN to alleviate his economic woes. See "For Sale," *Public Ledger* (Philadelphia, PA), August 25, 1855, 3.

18 "A New Steamboat on the Delaware," *Public Ledger* (Philadelphia, PA), May 19, 1857, 1.

19 With the success of the JOHN A. WARNER, the DRSC sold the THOMAS A. MORGAN to the Baltimore Steam Packet Company in April 1862 and the new owners transferred the MORGAN to the Chesapeake Bay. See "Steamer Thomas A. Morgan," *Philadelphia Inquirer*, April 28, 1862, 8.

20 "News from Fortress Monroe," *New York Times*, October 25, 1862, 1; "Fortress Monroe," *National Republican* (Washington, DC), May 27, 1861, 2.

21 Of note, during Cone and the WARNER's service during the war, the DRSC ceased operations on the Delaware until Cone's return. See "Shipping," *Philadelphia Inquirer*, June 8, 1865, 7.

22 See John Black, *Excursion on the Delaware: A History of Steamboats and Their Men in the Delaware Valley*, ed. Ruthe Baker (Woodbury: Gloucester County Historical Society, 1993), 196–209, 241–54; Charles Boyer, "Early Transportation Across the Delaware. A paper read at the Annual Meeting of the Gloucester County Historical Society, January 8, 1924." Unpublished manuscript. Gloucester County Historical Society, Woodbury, NJ.

23 See Emil Salvini, *Historic Cape May New Jersey: The Summer City by the Sea* (Charleston: The History Press, 2012); Joe Jordan, *Cape May Point: The Illustrated History, 1875 to the Present* (Atglen: Schiffer Publishing, 2003); Jeffery Dorwart, *Cape May County, New Jersey: The Making of an American Resort Community* (New Brunswick: Rutgers University Press, 1992).

24 See Martin Paulsson, *The Social Anxieties of Progressive Reform: Atlantic City, 1854–1920* (New York: New York University Press, 1994), 14–56; John Hall and George Bloodgood, *The Daily Union History of Atlantic City, New Jersey: Containing Sketches of the Past and Present of Atlantic City and County, With Maps and Illustrations Specially Prepared* (Atlantic City: Daily Union Printing Company, 1899), 11–36.

25 See Lorett Treese, *Railroads of New Jersey: Fragments of the Past in the Garden State Landscape* (Mechanisburg: Stackpole Books, 2006), 191–93; Dorwart, *Cape May County*, 93–99, 110–11.

26 Salvini, *Historic Cape May New Jersey*, 53.

27 When Cone and his business associates formed the DRSC, its charter read, in part: ". . . for establishing and maintaining a steamboat line for the conveyance of passengers, goods and merchandize [sic], on the river Delaware, or its tributary streams between Philadelphia and Bristol. . . ." In contrast, the charter of the new Delaware River Steamboat & Transportation Company included the following language: "The said Corporation has been formed for the purpose of operating steamboats and the conveyance of persons and freight thereon in the waters of the Delaware River and Bay." For the DRSC charter, see State of Pennsylvania, *Laws of the General Assembly of the State of Pennsylvania* (Harrisburg, PA: A. Boyd Hamilton, 1857), 364. For the DRS&TC charter, see State of Pennsylvania Charter Book no. 9, May 9, 1876, 565.

28 John W. Black, "Steamboats' Miscellany." Unpublished manuscript. Gloucester County Historical Society, Woodbury, NJ. Ordering a new steamboat from Harlan & Hollingsworth provided yet another rationale for forming the DRS&TC. Pleased with the just completed boat COLUMBIA, Cone and his associates signed a contract with the shipyard in September 1876 to build a "grand palace steamer" for the Philadelphia–Cape May run at a reported cost of $175,000. The new boat, named the REPUBLIC, was described as ". . . a new class of fast, side-wheel river steamboat. She was said to be beyond a doubt the finest river steamboat that had ever been on the Delaware." Launched in March and steamed from Wilmington up to Philadelphia on June 19, 1878, the next day the REPUBLIC sailed to her inaugural trip to Cape May with a crowd totaling 250 people, a mere ten percent of her stated capacity. The REPUBLIC would allow the DRS&TC to maintain a regular run between Philadelphia and Cape May while the WARNER serviced other ports.

29 Michael Chiarappa, "Play by the Bay: Recreation in Fortescue," *Down Jersey: From Bayshore to Seashore, a Guidebook for the Annual Conference of the Vernacular Architecture Forum*, ed. Robert Craig (Galloway: Richard Stockton University, 2014), 49–53; Margaret Louise Mints and Alex Ogden III, *Fortescue: The Weakfish Capital* (Port Norris: Margaret Louise Mints, 1996).

30 "Among the Jersey Phlebotamists," *The Morning Post* (Camden, NJ), September 5, 1878, 3; "Local Items," *Bridgeton Chronicle* (Bridgeton, NJ), February 16, 1877, 2.

31 "Local Items," *Bridgeton Chronicle*, May 18, 1877, 2. See also Bailey, "The Warner House at Sea Breeze, Part 1," 20.

32 For Lloyd's labors, see "Local Items," *Daily News* (Bridgeton, NJ), May 8, 1877, 2; for an early announcement of Sea Breeze see "New Route To The Sea" [advertisement], *The Philadelphia Inquirer* (Philadelphia, PA), September 8, 1877, 6.

33 "Local Items," *Bridgeton Chronicle*, April 13, 1877, 2.

34 "Local Items," *Bridgeton Chronicle*, June 1, 1877, 2; "Local Items," *Bridgeton Chronicle*, May 18, 1877, 2; "Local Items," *Bridgeton Chronicle*, February 16, 1877, 2.

35 Bailey, "The Warner House at Sea Breeze, Part 1," 21.

36 "The Warner House—Sea Breeze Island," *Bridgeton Chronicle*, July 20, 1877, 3; Bailey, "The Warner House at Sea Breeze, Part 1," 20–21.

37 David Scattergood, *The Delaware River Illustrated from Philadelphia to the Sea* (Philadelphia: David Scattergood, 1878), 16.

38 Black, *Excursion on the Delaware*, 215; Bailey, "The Warner House at Sea Breeze, Part 1," 21; "Local Items," *Bridgeton Chronicle*, June 28, 1878, 2; "Local Items," *Bridgeton Chronicle*, April 20, 1877, 2.

39 Until 1883, fares were 60 cents for adults per round-trip, children under 12 received half-price fares. See "Daily Excursions to Sea Breeze" [advertisement], *The Times* (Philadelphia, PA), August 12, 1884, 3.

40 "Sea Breeze," *Bridgeton Evening News*, August 12, 1884, 1; "Local Items," *Bridgeton Chronicle*, July 12, 1878, 2.

41 "Local Items," *Bridgeton Chronicle*, June 8, 1877, 2; Bailey, "The Warner House at Sea Breeze, Part 1," 21.

42 "Salt Water Day at Sea Breeze," [advertisement] *Bridgeton Evening News*, August 17, 1889, 4; "Grand Old-Fashioned Clam Bake" [advertisement], *The Times* (Philadelphia, PA), September 3, 1889, 4.

43 In South Jersey, local papers labeled the storm as the "Gale of 1878." See Kelvin Ramsey and Marijke Reilly, "The Hurricane of October 21–24, 1878," *Delaware Geological Society Special Publication* no. 22 (2002); Rick Schwartz, *Hurricanes and the Middle Atlantic States* (Springfield: Blue Diamond Books, 2007), 73; "The First Fall Gale," *Bridgeton Chronicle*, October 25, 1878, 1.

44 An 1879 inspector's report on storm damage to the lighthouse reads: "The storm of October 23, 1878, damaged this station greatly. Such repairs to the embankment as were necessary for the protection of the site have been made; but the structure was so much injured as to render the rebuilding of the lighthouse necessary." See "Cohansey Lighthouse Chronology," *Lighthouse Friends*, https://www.lighthousefriends.com/light.asp?ID=1884. For a lithographic depiction of the storm, see David Budlong Tyler, *The Bay and River Delaware: A Pictorial History* (Cambridge: Cornell Maritime Press, 1955), 123.

45 "Local News," *The Pioneer* (Bridgeton, NJ), February 13, 1879, 2.

46 "River Steamers," *Philadelphia Inquirer*, June 3, 1879, 1.

47 *Poor's Manual of Industrials – Seventh Annual Number* (New York: Poor's Manual Company, 1916), 1709–10; Cumberland County Deed Book 181: 435.

48 George Edward Reed, L.L.D., editor, *Pennsylvania Archives*, Fourth Series, vol. X, "Papers of the Governors, 1883–1891, Robert Emory Pattison" (Harrisburg, PA: State of Pennsylvania, William Stanley Ray, 1902), 45, 63.

49 At his trial in May 1877, authorities alleged Howard sold whiskey to at least one customer, Byron Bowen; see "Court Sentences," *Bridgeton Evening News*, May 12, 1887, 1. The Warner House had, however, apparently lost its license to sell malt liquor before February 1886. Whether the loss of the hotel's liquor license was due to the dissolution of the DRS&TC is uncertain. See "Good Times Ahead for the Tavern at Deerfield," *The Pioneer*, February 4, 1886, 9.

50 See "Sea Breeze" [advertisement], *Courier-Post* (Camden, NJ), July 21, 1885, 4.

51 See "News Notes," *Bridgeton Evening News*, August 30, 1889, 2; "Excursion to Sea Breeze," *Delaware County Times* (Chester, PA), August 6, 1886, 2.

52 "Cool and Pleasant" [advertisement], *The Times* (Philadelphia, PA), August 24, 1889, 4; "Summer Ramblings," *Courier-Post* (Camden, NJ), July 25, 1888, 4.

53 "The Warner House," *Bridgeton Evening News*, May 20, 1889, 2.

54 "Warner House Destroyed," *Bridgeton Pioneer*, April 17, 1890, 6; Bailey, "The Warner House at Sea Breeze, Part 1," 21.

55 "The Warner House to Be Rebuilt," *Bridgeton Evening News*, April 18, 1890, 1.

56 "News Notes," *Bridgeton Evening News*, May 28, 1890, 2.

57 "John A. Warner" [advertisement], *The Times* (Philadelphia, PA), June 27, 1890, 2.

58 "Down to Sea Breeze" [advertisement], *Philadelphia Inquirer*, June 29, 1890, 7.

59 "Afternoon Excursions Up the Delaware" [advertisement], *Philadelphia Inquirer*, June 27, 1891, 8; "Daily and Sunday Excursions on the Magnificent Palace Steamer Columbia" [advertisement], *Philadelphia Inquirer*, June 27, 1890, 2.

60 "Excursions" [advertisement], *The Times* (Philadelphia, PA), August 1, 1891, 6.

61 "Will It Be Re—Built?" *Bridgeton Pioneer*, December 10, 1891, 2.

62 "An Active Life Ended," *Philadelphia Inquirer*, October 11, 1887, 2.

63 Shirley Bailey and Jim Parkhurst, *Early South Jersey Amusement Parks* (Millville: South Jersey Publishing, 1979); Oliver Sheets, "About Lincoln Park," unpublished manuscript, Amusement Parks Collection, Gloucester County Historical Society, Woodbury, NJ; see also Black, *Excursion on the Delaware*, 241–54.

64 Black, *Excursion on the Delaware*, 203–10; Henry Pincus, *Picturesque Washington Park on the Delaware* (Philadelphia: Henry Pincus, 1896).

65 "Sale by Receivers of Lincoln Park and Steamboat Consolidated Co.," *The Constitution* (Woodbury, NJ), May 5, 1897, 1 ; "Master's Sale of Real Estate and Personal Property, Germania Park!" *The Constitution*, November 4, 1896, 3.

66 "The Storm at Sea Breeze," *Dollar Weekly News* (Bridgeton, NJ), November 1, 1890, 2.

67 "At Sea Breeze," *Bridgeton Evening News*, July 25, 1893, 2.

68 "Life Among Our Neighbors," *Bridgeton Evening News*, August 18, 1900, 2.

69 "Little Locals," *Bridgeton Evening News*, June 6, 1890, 2.

70 "Sea Breeze," *Bridgeton Pioneer*, July 30, 1896, 2.

71 "Concerning Sea Breeze . . . to the Editor," *Bridgeton Evening News*, September 4, 1899, 2.

72 Elliot, *The Saga of the Wilson Line*, 17; "Merry River War On," *Trenton Evening Times*, June 17, 1901, 1. For the reorganization, see "Arrow Shots at Home News,"

Bridgeton Evening News, July 10, 1900, 4.

73 Cumberland County Deed Book 291: 314.

74 When Lloyd died, his passing was front-page news in Bridgeton. Memorialized as a veteran of the Civil War, the paper, noting a recent fire at the Lloyd family home, urged readers: "This is an opportunity for showing the neighborly kindness which is real charity and all who want to help may send contributions" to support Lloyd's family. See "Death of George Lloyd," *Bridgeton Evening News*, November 8, 1915, 1.

75 See "Picnic At Sea Breeze," *Bridgeton Evening News*, July 27, 1912, 6; "Sea Breeze," *Bridgeton Evening News*, June 29, 1911, 6.

76 "New Jersey Property" [classified ad], *Philadelphia Inquirer*, March 17, 1918, 19.

77 Cumberland County Deed Book 363: 88.

78 Whether Wise had a map prepared for his Sea Breeze subdivision is uncertain as such a map has not turned up in multiple searches of the Cumberland County Clerk's office. Bailey mentions a survey conducted by Furman Sheppard, a highway surveyor and township property assessor from Cedarville, but she did not cite a source for that claim. See Bailey, "The Warner House at Sea Breeze, Part 2," 31.

79 "'Sea Breeze' To Be Revived," *Bridgeton Evening News*, May 4, 1918, 3.

80 "Sea Breeze, Subdivision on the Delaware Bay" [advertisement], *Bridgeton Evening News*, May 4, 1918, 6.

81 "They Drew Fine Lots at Movies, With a String," *Chicago Tribune*, June 19, 1918, 3.

82 Wise's agents canvased movie theaters in Chicago and possibly Detroit. Before each motion picture, the targeted theaters showed a slide announcing a lottery for land in Michigan. After receiving a moviegoer's contact information, agents followed up, if possible, with a phone call followed by a visit to the "winner's" home. Agents informed the individual of their prize, for which they would have to pay $2.80 to the visiting agent in order to secure their prize, go to the AIA's offices to select a lot, and, finally, pay $7 to $14 to cover the cost of transferring the title. See also reporting in "Prize Winners Pay $11 for $1 Lots," *The Times* (Munster, IN), June 20, 1918, 2.

83 Two years before the raid, Chicago lawyer Geary Stighen hired the AIA as realtors for two tracts of land in Muskegon County, Michigan; Stighen allegedly received the second tract from a farmer in exchange for a used car. The company divided the property into small lots and, despite no body of water nearby, called the venture "Lakeview Terrace." See "Says $150 Tract Sold For $10,000," *Grand Rapids Press* (Grand Rapids, MI), November 24, 1917, 3; "Movie Patrons Get Prizes of Muskegon Land," *Muskegon Chronicle* (Muskegon, MI), November 27, 1917, 12; "Plan of Movies in Lot Selling Hits Muskegon," *Muskegon Chronicle*, October 14, 1916, 7; "Those 'Summer Homes for the Poor,'" *Chicago Tribune*, October 13, 1916, 12.

84 "Try Alleged Land Sharks," *Philadelphia Inquirer*, June 27, 1918, 8; "Shore Realty Dealer is Wanted in Chicago," *Philadelphia Inquirer*, June 20, 1918, 8.

85 *North American* (Philadelphia, PA), June 15, 1918, reprinted in Bailey, "The Warner House at Sea Breeze, Part 2," 31–32.

86 "Township of Fairfield Notice of Tax Sale," *Bridgeton Evening News*, August 5, 1919, 3. A report from Chancery court identified Sea Breeze properties subject to tax sale belonging to Joseph Wise and 28 Philadelphia residents. Identifiable purchasers ranged from working-class immigrants to residents of Philadelphia's middle-class neighborhoods. See "In Chancery Court of New Jersey," *Bridgeton Evening News*, September 19, 1922.

87 Albert W. Kauffmann v. Joseph Wise et al., Chancery of New Jersey, 52/207-2033 (January 3, 1923).

88 Cumberland County Deed Book 405: 433.

89 William Cauthorn had multiple business interests in Greenwich. He had owned a general store at the Greenwich Piers on the Cohansey and ran an event hall and movie theater with a nearby ice cream parlor and pool room. His interests did not, however, include real estate investments other than Sea Breeze.

90 Residents Arthur Sooy, Frank Dilsworth, Winfield Fisher, Rufus S. Richards, and Percival Wilson registered a deed on November 6, 1929, for 8,000 square feet in Sea Breeze. Whether they built a clubhouse on the property is uncertain as they sold the property in 1934. See Cumberland County Deed Book 469: 255; and Cumberland County Deed Book 474: 342.

91 According to local oral tradition, Smith was a one-armed teetotaler and muskrat trapper. When Harry Griffith moved with his family to Sea Breeze in 1927 and opened the Sea Breeze Tavern, known as New Jersey's least-molested prohibition-era speakeasy, relations between Smith and the gregarious and sometimes ill-mannered Griffith were tense, at best. See Don E. Woods, "Seabreeze: The Lost History of a Once Thriving 19th Century N.J. Beach Resort," *NJ.com*, https://www.nj.com/cumberland/2017/03/seabreeze_the_lost_history_of_a_once_thriving_19th.html; Bailey, "The Warner House at Sea Breeze, Part 2," 32; Virgil Johnson, "Ramblin' Round," *Millville Daily* (Millville, NJ), May 28, 1974, 4.

92 Henry Beck, "Fairton Church Marks Site of Old Fairfield," *Courier-Post* (Camden, NJ), August 17, 1930, 17.

93 For the Seabreeze Hotel fire, see: "Sea Breeze Hotel Destroyed By Fire," *Daily Journal* (Vineland, NJ), January 23, 1942, 8. By 1940, Cauthorn sold 17 lots in Sea Breeze. The deed for his earliest Sea Breeze sale, to the Sea Breeze Rod and Gun Club, mentions the property was along "Beach Avenue"; whether the road was surveyed for Cauthorn or was a holdover from Wise's hiring of Furman Sheppard is uncertain.

94 Dan Walsh, "Owners Agree to Sell Sea Breeze Homes to State as Delaware Bay Eats Away at Another Town," *Press of Atlantic City*, May 8, 2010, https://www.pressofatlanticcity.com/news/press/cumberland/owners-agree-to-sell-sea-breeze-homes-to-state-as/article_c54de1dc-5a2a-11df-863a-001cc4c002e0.html.

95 Jason Nark, "Failing Seawall Threatens 'A Way of Life,'" *Philadelphia Daily News*, August 8, 2009, 6, 7. While area newspapers, the State of New Jersey, Fairfield Township officials, and residents referred to the barrier as a "sea wall," the arch-like design of the barrier's interlocking concrete blocks is a design common to revetments.

96 NJDEP [New Jersey Department of Environmental Protection]. 2020. "Blue Acres Floodplain Acquisitions." https://www.state.nj.us/dep/greenacres/blue_flood_ac.html. See also "New Jersey's Blue Acres is Well-Run Part of a Small Response to Flood Risk," *Press of Atlantic City*, October 18, 2019; "Governor Christie Announces Expansion of Successful Blue Acres Program to Protect More New Jersey Homeowners," Office of the Governor New Release, October 23, 2017; Christopher Flavelle, "A New Strategy for Climate Change? Retreat," *Bloomberg News*, August 22, 2016, https://www.bloomberg.com/opinion/articles/2016-08-22/nj-s-blue-acres-program-a-new-strategy-for-climate-change.

97 As the Delaware Bay and conservation programs, including the Blue Acres program, transform Sea Breeze and other Bayshore communities, the need for recording the stories of these communities is of critical importance. Therefore, to echo Shirley Bailey, if anyone has information on the people named in this article, records of the various incarnations of the Delaware River Steamboat Company, or letters or ephemera from vacations at the Warner House or any era of Sea Breeze, I would appreciate hearing from you. Hopefully, someone could help fill in the missing pieces.

Junk Put Police Chief to Shame

Merchantville's Popular Officer Feels Humiliated Because Prisoner Broke Out of Jail

Special to The Inquirer.

MERCHANTVILLE, N. J., March 30. — For the first time in his official career of fifteen years Chief of Police Linderman is suffering the humiliation of having one of his prisoners escape from the cell in which the chief locked him. Linderman blames it all on the Merchantville Water Company, which is having a standpipe erected a hundred feet from the borough jail. The latter boasts of two cells, made of heavy planks and grated iron doors. Yesterday morning a man, who gave the name of Vincent Omaya, fell into the chief's hands. The man had a bag full of junk and some plumbers' tools, that looked as though they had been stolen.

When Linderman visited the jail shortly after noon to see that a meal from a restaurant was given the prisoner the cell was empty. The prisoner had a friend on the outside. The friend, sheltered by a narrow alley, had climbed to a window, knocked it out and passed a crowbar to the prisoner. Outside the bang, bang, of the riveters on the standpipe prevented the noise made by the prisoner smashing the door being heard until he could wrench off the lock. Once out of the cell it was simply a case of turning the deadlatch in the outer door and leaving.

The prisoner gave an address on Lombard street, Philadelphia, but he is not known there. Linderman says he knows where to get him and will have him in a day or two. The contents of the bag await identification in the station house.

The Philadelphia Inquirer, Sunday Morning, March 31, 1907.

Maurice River Fire Deals Serious Damage to Oyster Houses

Images from the Mickey Smith Collection; text by Louis Burgess

The West Jersey & Seashore Railroad's Maurice River Oyster Sheds, located across from Bivalve, New Jersey, prior to their fiery destruction.

A fire ignited in the West Jersey & Seashore's ticket office at its Maurice River oyster facility, located across from the Bivalve oyster sheds, around 10 p.m. on March 27, 1907. The fire soon engulfed the oyster wharves, crowded with dozens of packing and shipping houses.[1] Powell Garrison, a clerk in Joseph Garrison's grocery store, who was asleep on the premises, was awakened by the fire and "had to make his escape through a window. He did not have time to even get on a coat."[2] Due to a lack of firefighting equipment on-site, onlookers were helpless to intervene; authorities failed to identify the cause of the fire. Several men braved the flames to unmoor valuable oyster vessels tied to the burning docks and set them afloat downriver. None suffered damage, but the men involved claimed to have had a "thrilling experience."[3] As the fire progressed, the oyster floats along the wharves (which received oysters unloaded from schooners before they were transferred to scows) caught fire and were also cut loose to float away from the docks. One account described them colliding with the already drifting oyster schooners; the crews onboard had to work hard to keep the boats from being seriously damaged. "The

Workers hoisting baskets of oysters from a scow to the wharf for packing into burlap bags at Bivalve, across from the WJ&S's Maurice River oyster facility.

spectacle was a beautiful one as the drifting burning floats cast fantastic shadows upon the black waters."[4]

After some time, a ferry tugboat owned by the West Jersey Railroad Company arrived on the scene and helped to slow the fire by pumping water between the buildings.[5] Unfortunately, "all of the buildings were built over the water on pilings and the plank wharves burned as freely and fiercely as did the buildings."[6] While estimates of damage to the oyster houses and surrounding buildings varied, the losses were projected to be from $35,000 to $50,000.[7] Further assessments of the damage led owners to claim it "will cost a third more than when it was built to replace property."[8] Of the dozens of oyster houses in this bustling maritime center, only a small number, from five to seven, were spared from the blaze. Luckily, no one was injured in the fire.

When the conflagration ended, Hearn and Company, grocers and ship chandlers, had lost stock, office furnishings, papers, books, and documents in the fire. The shipping houses of Bateman and Blizzard, Furman Demaris, Ogden Gandy, Henry & Buzby, Maurice Rogers & Co., G. C. Yates, William L. Fidler, Hagemant & Pole, and John Gaskill all suffered damage and destruction.[9] Despite the heavy losses, Hearn and Company were advertising less than a month later, on April 22, that they would "run a temporary place of business there while their new store is being built."[10]

The State Oyster Commission office, stationed at the docks and also destroyed, had been equipped with a fire-proof safe that plunged into the Maurice River as the flooring upon which it stood disintegrated in the fire. Its most valuable documents were recovered a week later when the safe was lifted out of the river: "The books were wet and the bindings loosened, so that they will have to be rebound, but the records were found to be legible and intact."[11]

The West Jersey & Seashore Railroad, the insured owner of the wharves and burned buildings, led the reconstruction effort, overseen by R. H. Pinkham. Within two weeks "section gangs" were sent to the area to begin reconstruction—the work was "pushed as rapidly as possible." The rebuilt docks and oyster sheds were equipped with "all the conveniences for shipping the famous bivalves of the Maurice River."[12] The new structures were built in accordance with improved regulations and fire prevention measures to ensure such a disaster would not occur again.

Oyster sloops and schooners at rest on the Maurice River looking towards the Central Railroad of New Jersey's Bivalve oyster sheds.

Another view of workers lifting baskets of oysters from a scow up to the wharf for packing.

The images in this article are from the Mickey Smith Cumberland County postcard collection. We thank him for allowing their use here.

This oyster schooner's crew is preparing their boat for a night of rest after working the oyster beds all day. The WJ&S's Maurice River oyster sheds can be seen in the background, along with the ferry tugboat West Jersey crossing the river.

A crowd of gawkers line the shore examining the smoldering ruins of the WJ&S's Maurice River oyster sheds. The platform seen on the left side of the photograph was used to move the oysters into boxcars.

The photograph above shows the fire's aftermath: piles of burnt wood and twisted corrugated iron sheet roofing. The building in the background center appears to be a single-stall engine house to maintain a locomotive at this facility.

Work crews have already removed much of the wreckage from atop the pilings, revealing just how devastating the fire was to the facility.

About the Author

Louis "Bud" Burgess is a graduating senior at Stockton University, Class of '20, majoring in Communications. Having transferred to Stockton in 2018, Bud has continued to hone his writing through meaningful classes and conversations. He plans to capture his creativity, with a goal of storyboarding, writing novels, and improvisational storytelling, as he finds his path as a creator.

Endnotes

1 "Fire Sweeps Maurice River," *Bridgeton Pioneer* (Bridgeton, NJ), April 4, 1907, 1.
2 "Fire Sweeps Maurice River," *Bridgeton Pioneer*, April 4, 1907, 1.
3 "Fire Sweeps Maurice River," *Bridgeton Pioneer*, April 4, 1907, 1.
4 "Fire Sweeps Maurice River," *Bridgeton Pioneer*, April 4, 1907, 1.
5 "Disastrous Fire At Maurice River," *Bridgeton Evening News* (Bridgeton, NJ), March 30, 1907, 1.
6 "Fire Sweeps Maurice River," *Bridgeton Pioneer*, April 4, 1907, 1.
7 "Disastrous Fire at Maurice River," *Bridgeton Evening News*, March 30, 1901, 2; "Maurice River Fire Loss is Heavy," *Bridgeton Evening News*, April 1, 1901, 1; "Blaze at Maurice River," *Trenton Sunday Advertiser* (Trenton, NJ), March 31, 1907, 7.
8 "Maurice River Fire Loss Is Heavy," *Bridgeton Evening News*, April 1, 1907, 1.
9 "Disastrous Fire At Maurice River," *Bridgeton Evening News*, March 30, 1907, 2; "Flames in Oyster District," *The Philadelphia Inquirer*, March 31, 1907, 22.
10 "Ready for Business," *Bridgeton Evening News*, April 22, 1907, 1.
11 "Safes Hauled from Bottom of River," *The Philadelphia Inquirer*, April 9, 1907, 3.
12 "Repairing Wharves," *Millville Evening News* (Millville, NJ), April 12, 1907, 1.

With the fire extinguished, WJ&S linemen, standing on a platform constructed on the roof of an old combine passenger car, are busy restringing new telegraph wires to bring the branch line back to full train operations.

Forgotten South Jersey Author:
His Stories of the Pine Barrens

F. James Bergmann

This article is one of many that could be written about George Agnew Chamberlain, a largely forgotten South Jersey author who lived and wrote during the twentieth century. From the 1920s to the 1960s, he resided in the quaint town of Quinton in Salem County, New Jersey. In 1927, Chamberlain purchased Lloyd's Landing on the Alloways Creek. His home has its own unique place in history. From there he researched and wrote about the people and places he came to love in what Chamberlain called the Barrens. He died in 1966.

Though not originally from New Jersey—he was born in San Paulo, Brazil, in 1879—he came to America in 1891 to continue his education. Chamberlain attended several private and one public school during his youth. As a young adult he graduated from Lawrenceville School in Mercer County, New Jersey, and went on to attend Princeton for two years. In 1902, he returned to Brazil to teach, sell religious books, and, finally, join the consular service. It was also at this time he began to write and have his stories published. He came back to America for a short time and then returned to Brazil as the Consul General in Pernambuco. From Brazil he was assigned to Lourenco Marques in Portuguese East Africa and from there to Mexico City, Mexico. He resigned from the service in 1919 to write full time.

George Agnew Chamberlain, 1926.

Chamberlain was not living in South Jersey in 1923 when he wrote and self published his first South Jersey story, *Highboy Rings Down the Curtain*. It is about Highboy, a horse who met with a tragic end and the people who trained and admired him. The story was first published in the *Saturday Evening Post* in December 1922 and then republished, in expanded form, by the Bridgeton Evening News in a limited edition of 300 copies. Though short in length, it was featured in *New Stories for Men* in 1943 and *Great Horse Stories* in 1948.[1]

Chamberlain was in Africa in 1914. While there, he was a member of the Circumnavigators Club started by John H. Birch Jr. of Burlington, New Jersey. John Jr. was the son of John H. Birch Sr., and the grandson of Thomas Harrison Birch who in 1863 founded a company in Burlington that produced carriages, harnesses, and sleighs on Library

A Son and Daughter Upset in Portuguese East Africa

Two weeks ago my launch was held up in the mouth of the Maputo River by a southerly buster, forty-six kilometers from home. There is a government post there and a road without a turn that leads thence hitherward across a bald wilderness. As I was accompanied by a certain Leading Lady it was absolutely essential that we reach a chaperone by nightfall. The government post offered me a mule and a little two-wheeled buggy.

The government post said: "You and the lady get in first—then we hitch the mule." . . . When she was securely hitched to the buggy the government post said: "She runs perfectly straight; so does the road. I'll telephone ahead for them to stop her when you get there. Luck to you—" . . .

That mule was certainly imbued with the American spirit of hustle. We had 46 kilometers to go, but she began looking for the end of the road at once. Mule, Lady and Self soon got accustomed to each other and as it was a government road with white kilometer posts painted with big black numerals it was easy to keep track and to figure that we were going to make a record passage.

I was holding the reins. At high noon we passed a kilometer post and I asked, "What does it say?"

"Twenty-three," said the Leading Lady, and the next minute I felt the whole body of the cart sink backwards. By hanging onto one line with all my might I got the mule running in a circle on the veldt and told the Leading Lady to ask no questions but jump. She did, and then I did. For two minutes the mule and the cart and self did a pin-wheel figure that beat anything in the modern dances. The mule and the cart got all the skin off my left thigh, but I finally got the mule's goat and held it while the Leading Lady, who was pure nerve, unhitched. There wasn't a hut or a tree . . . in sight; only bare veldt and the middle of twenty miles of straight road. So the Lady had to hold the mule while I examined the damage.

It was a hopeless case. Two stays and four bolts had given away. The body of the cart was just balanced on the shafts and the shafts balanced on the axle. I groaned and reported to the Fair; then my eye fell on the step of the cart, where was written a Name and a Place. I reeled.

"Heavens!" cried the L. L., "What's the matter now?"

"Matter!" I yelled, "the chap that made this damned cart is a FRIEND of mine!"

Lourenco, Marquez, Port. E. Africa.
Nov. 12, 1914.

Street. The business began purely for home trade. It remained local until the Boston Fruit Company wanted carts made "to be taken back to the West Indies in their empty banana steamers running out of Philadelphia."[2] Word spread and orders began to arrive from all over the globe. This led to sending Jinrikishes (rickshaws) to Japan, India, Madagascar and South Africa. During the Transvaal war, both the Boers and British used Birch wagons as did the Japanese and Russians in Manchuria. Notably, the American and Spaniards used British wagons during the Spanish-American war.

John H. Birch Sr. was appointed by President Wilson to the post as the U.S. Minister Plenipotentiary to the Kingdom of Portugal in 1915.[3] He and Chamberlain knew each other. John H. Birch Jr., who worked for the family business, also edited the magazine called *The Log of the Circumnavigators Club*. The members of the club came from varied backgrounds. One member was Chamberlain.

While still in Africa, Chamberlain wrote an article that appeared in *The Log* where is said, "Circumamericanconsulchamberlain joins the contributors to the Sunset Series Around the World."[4] His contribution was "A Son and Daughter Upset in Portuguese East Africa." Read the excerpted story in the sidebar. The friend and cart maker mentioned at the end of the story was none other than John H. Birch Jr.

Chamberlain appeared twice in *The Log* in 1922. The first mention was about his novel *Home* (1914) that was being made into a movie. The director was Louis J. Gasnier and it was produced by R. C. Pictures. The movie title was *The Call of Home*. It was Chamberlain's third silent movie.[5] The same issue mentioned his new romance story "Pot of Gold."[6] His final appearance in *The Log* was in 1927. It told that Chamberlain and A. E. Thomas had written the play *Lost* that opened at the Mansfield Theater; Rollo Lloyd directed and Ramsey Wallace was the producer.[7] The play was based on his novel *Home*.[8] The Birch family and Chamberlain were lifelong friends and had many other mutual involvements over the years.

"Jarrad, Last of the Pineys"

In his foreword to William C. Bolger's *Smithville: The Result of Enterprise*, Henry Bisbee, county historian for Burlington County, New Jersey, mentions Chamberlain. Bisbee describes an article about Smithville written by local historian Nathaniel Ewan, which was rejected for publication by the *Lincoln-Mercury Times*. The magazine, it was reported, wanted a *name writer* and had engaged Chamberlain to write an article in place of Ewan:

> Chamberlain had never heard of Smithville but he interviewed the present Smith clan there. They of course fed him a one-sided story. Chamberlain built a fantastic article which the publisher turned down by reason of its utter improbability.[9]

Referring to the life of Hezekiah B. Smith, Bisbee writes in his foreword, "The plot cries for an author such as George Agnew Chamberlain, who thrilled me as a boy when I devoured his stories in the old *Saturday Evening Post*."[10] Unfortunately, the text of Chamberlain's rejected article has not been found. It was not among the family papers read by this author. Bisbee presents a tantalizing thought of what might have been: "Indeed, Chamberlain might have considered writing a novel about Smithville . . ." if his shorter study had made it into print.

One of the stories Chamberlain wrote in the *Post* in 1925 was "Jarrad, Last of the Pineys." To write this story he traveled to the Pine Barrens to study its people and land. He traveled there in his convertible. At the time he wrote "Jarrad," Chamberlain listed his address as 99 W. Commerce Street, Bridgeton, New Jersey. This was his mother's home since 1906 when she moved back from Brazil.

In the story he writes that the Pine Barrens are the "stronghold of the Pineys"; they live in "houses, like you and me, and are just as good as you and me." Contrary to some accounts they are not "savages" or "wild men of the woods," or speak an "unintelligible tongue."[11] After the story appeared, L. H. Patterson, a writer for the *Newark Evening News*, sent a letter to Chamberlain, writing, "You have the psychology of the pines absolutely true"; he remarks that this is the "best and truest Piney story . . . ."[12] Patterson went on to write that Chamberlain should get into the *Best Short Stories of 1925* publication, as the piece was a masterpiece.[13] Patterson also agreed with him that the Pineys were a "much maligned people" but that "Jarrad is a photographic portrait of a mentality so sharply outlined as to be vitally affecting."[14] Chamberlain responded to Patterson on June 15 but sadly a copy of his reply has not been found.

In Chamberlain's assessment of the Pine Barrens, he wrote you could ride miles on end with no people or houses until suddenly the "houses are there; some of them hidden, others looming suddenly in a clearing cluttered with barns, sheds, flowers and an astonishing growth of vegetables."[15] When you "enter one of them, study it, and you may discover, embedded amid its rooms and covered on the outside with sheathing the original one-room log cabin which brought the forgotten Pineys into lurid fame."[16]

Chamberlain carefully describes the houses in his stories and novels. In one of his unpublished South Jersey stories he tells the reader to

> . . . leave out the classic colonial and put your mind on the patch-work house of the patch-quilt period. Some cobbler or wheelwright would erect a cube of stone, make money and breed children, add a wing of brick, shove out a shingled porch here and a penthouse there and brighten his main fanlight with the warped wink of a bull's-eye glass.[17]

He is able to paint a picture in the reader's mind's eye with his descriptive words. His words come alive and provide a visual portrait of the place he was writing about.

See if the following passages from "Jarrad" do this for you. Chamberlain describes Jarrad's life in several seasons in the Pine Barrens.

> On the sunny days of spring he gathered swamp moss, valuable to florists and packers of fine crockery, laid it out to dry; and when he had accumulated the equivalent of a bail, hitched up the mule that lived contentedly on hay in a lean-to at one end of the cabin, and drove to the crossroads at Two Heads.[18]

In the summer Jarrad picked blueberries by hand and

> none knew better than he where to find the swamp shrubs which yielded the largest and bluest fruit. It was a joy to fill his pail with big berries all of one color—a blue as pale, deep and soft as the edge of the evening sky.[19]

Fall meant the cranberry harvest and

> Jarrad's minute knowledge of the woods and every hidden bottom from the headwaters of Cedar Creek to the gurgling course of the Pennypot stood him in good stead. He knew

> of strayed bushes in forgotten mudholes far withdrawn from the ken of their rightful owners.[20]

As a lifelong South Jersey resident, except for a few years in Maine, I have experienced first hand the places Chamberlain describes—they are real, beautiful and exciting.

Midnight Boy

Henry Charlton Beck first described Weymouth in the late 1930s. His description was based on the 1834 history of New Jersey by Thomas Francis Gordon. Beck wrote, "Weymouth was described as a blast furnace, forge and village in Hamilton Township, Gloucester County, upon the Great Egg Harbour River, about five minutes above the head of navigation."[21] He wrote that the village also contained "a grist mill and saw mill, and buildings for the workmen, of whom 100 are constantly employed about the works, and the persons depending upon them for subsistence average about 600 annually."[22] When Beck visited in the 1930s, he observed there were only a few "old houses along the stream and back in the green jungle, only a tall brick chimney, with a tuft of grass growing high at the top."[23]

Chamberlain had been to the Pines in the 1920s when he wrote "Jarrad." He returned in the 1940s to write a sequel to the first Lassie picture for MGM. He and several other writers had been hired to write the script for the movie. He was paid $5,000 up-front whether they accepted it or not. MGM rejected his story. In a letter to the editor at MGM, Chamberlain wanted to know "whether the *Lassie* project was abandoned because my synopsis seemed louzy . . . ."[24] No response to his inquiry has been found.

Whether it was "louzy" or not, Chamberlain now contacted the *Saturday Evening Post* with his story. After several revisions and negotiations over how much he would be paid, he received a letter from the *Post* in which the editor Ben Hibbs agreed the *Post* would pay him $30,000 for the serial, which they explained to Chamberlain was "pretty close to our top price for

George Agnew Chamberlain in his punt on Alloways Creek with Buff.

serials and somewhat higher than we pay many of our regulars such as Bob Carson, Earl Stanley Gardiner, Leslie Ford, Phil Wylie, et al."[25]

One might ask the question why he chose to use the Pine Barrens as the place to stage the *Lassie* sequel. It had been two decades since he wrote about the Pineys. Whatever his reason was, it produced a great serial and novel, titled *Midnight Boy*. Where did this title come from? Seems the lead character's name was Mark Perry, who was born at midnight and therefore forever lucky! You take a journey with Mark to Tolyer Knoll in the region where "... deer play around all year long, until they crash wide-eyed into slaughter" from the guns of illegal hunters. Chamberlain called Chatsworth the "legendary capital of the Pines" and Atsion a factory town that once supplied "cannons for General George Washington." He also described the area as having "districts where the law is loath to enter" and any law officer who would "crash bullheaded into an illicit deer killing in the Pines would be mourned not as a hero but as one whose brain hadn't been working right."

As the story develops and the main characters approached the main house in Weymouth, Chamberlain describes it as a "frame house, enormous, and with one corner rising in a squared tower four stories high. A roofed veranda surrounded the ground floor and there was one above it, roofless, but guarded by a carved balustrade." The drawing of the house that accompanied the *Saturday Evening Post* serial matches a 1940s photograph of the Weymouth house. Chamberlain wrote that, as you enter the house and once inside the front door, the "blackness of the musty hall was like pushing your face into the soft side of carbon paper." As you ascend the main stairway to the third floor, there was a "labyrinth of chopped-up rooms, each with an open door, each with a staring window." On the outside around the house there was a "faded path" that led to a "brick smokestack sixty feet high." There were also "low arches, under which rushed the raceway . . . walls of stone three feet thick broke off short or raised jagged teeth towards the sky." From a "buttressed escarpment" you could look down into walls that "formed squares, oblongs and even a nest of vats, each with a narrow rectangular opening like a door."[26]

The story centers around Mark uncovering the mystery of his past and how Tolyer Knoll played a role. There are colorful locals, a young girl, a dog and illegal deer hunting. This is Chamberlain's only novel about this region of South Jersey. Most of his other South Jersey works involve Salem and Cumberland counties. Like many of his novels, *Midnight Boy* was translated into foreign languages.

George Agnew Chamberlain deserves another look in the twenty-first century. His stories and novels open windows into South Jersey communities that present surprising, but recognizable detail. While some of these communities are gone, and all are certainly changed, they are the predecessors to our communities today. Within Chamberlain's stories, readers can find aspects of South Jersey history. How we preserve and view such history says much about our current understanding of the world.

Colwell Manor, the main house in Weymouth. Stephen Colwell constructed his country seat in 1865. The drawing in the *Saturday Evening Post* is modeled upon this house.

About the Author

Jim Bergman grew up in Glassboro, New Jersey, attended Glassboro High School, Glassboro State College (Rowan), Temple and Rutgers. He taught Special Education and Alternative Education classes and was the first principal of Cumberland County Vocational-Technical Center. He relocated to Maine, where he lived in Alna for sixteen years; he is the author of the book *The Narrow Gauge Railroad in Alna Maine* (2009). Since his retirement in 2000, he has been able to collect and write about various subjects. He resides in Upper Deerfield Township and is currently working on a biography of George Agnew Chamberlain.

Endnotes

1 *Saturday Evening Post*, 195, no. 27 (December 30, 1922), 6–7, 54, 56. *New Stories For Men*, ed. Charles Grayson (Garden City, NY: Garden City Publishing Co., 1943), 55–75. *Great Horse Stories*, ed. Page Cooper (Garden City, NY: Doubleday & Co., 1948) 146–69.

2 *Scannell's New Jersey First Citizens: Biographies and Portraits of. . .*, vol. 1, eds. William Edgar Sackett, John James Scannell (Paterson, NJ: J. J. Scannell, 1917).

3 Ibid.

4 *The Log of the Circumnavigators Club*, ed. John H. Birch, 4, no. 3 (December–January 1914–15), 23.

5 *The Log of the Circumnavigators Club*, ed. John H. Birch, 12, no. 2 (November–December 1922), 29.

6 Ibid., 37.

7 The Mansfield Theatre opened in 1926 at 256 W. 47th Street, New York City. The theatre was designed by Herbert J. Krapp, funded by the Chanin brothers, and named for the late actor Richard Mansfield, who died in 1907. The venue was renamed for *New York Times* theatre critic Brooks Atkinson in 1960. These details taken from *Playbill*: https://www.playbill.com/venue/mansfield-theatre-vault-0000000266.

8 *The Log of the Circumnavigators Club*, ed. John H. Birch, 16, no. 4 (March–April 1927), 51.

9 William C. Bolger, *Smithville: The Result of Enterprise* (Burlington County Cultural & Heritage Commission, 1990), xiii.

10 Ibid.

11 George Agnew Chamberlain, "Jarrad, Last of the Pineys," *Saturday Evening Post*, 197, no. 48 (May 30, 1925), 3–5, 31–38.

12 L. H. Patterson, *The Newark Evening News* (1925).

13 Ibid.

14 Ibid.

15 "Jarrad, Last of the Pineys."

16 Ibid.

17 George Agnew Chamberlain, "Sprague's Stopping," unpublished manuscript, 1940s. Family papers.

18 "Jarrad, Last of the Pineys."

19 Ibid.

20 Ibid. "Jarrad, Last of the Pineys" was published in the May 30, 1925, issue of the *Saturday Evening Post*. The story enters the public domain in 2021; we hope to publish it in the summer 2021 issue of *SoJourn*.

21 Henry Charlton Beck, *More Forgotten Towns of Southern New Jersey* (New Brunswick, NJ: Rutgers University Press, 1937), 283. Thomas Francis Gordon, *Gazetteer of the State of New Jersey* (Trenton, NJ: Daniel Fenton Publisher, 1834; reprinted, Cottonport, LA: Polyanthos Inc., 1973 [preface by Donald A. Sinclair]), 263.

22 Gordon, ibid., 263.

23 Beck, *More Forgotten Towns*, 288.

24 George Agnew Chamberlain, Letter to MGM, Lloyd's Landing, Quinton, New Jersey, September 15, 1948. Family papers.

25 Ben Hibbs, editor, Letter from *Saturday Evening Post*, September 1, 1948. Family papers.

26 All quotations in this paragraph are from George Agnew Chamberlain, *Midnight Boy* (New York: The Bobbs-Merrill Company, Inc., 1949), 27.

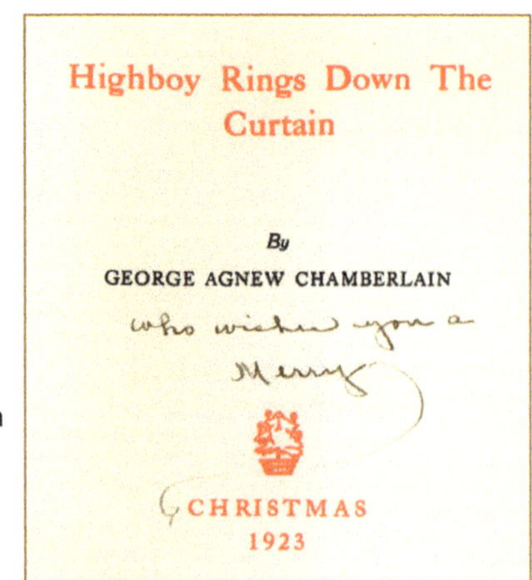

Highboy Rings Down The Curtain

By

GEORGE AGNEW CHAMBERLAIN

who wishes you a Merry

CHRISTMAS

1923

Chamberlain was not living in South Jersey when he wrote his first South Jersey story, *Highboy Rings Down The Curtain*. (Right) From the title page of the Christmas 1923 edition, with Chamberlain's greetings, published by the Evening News Company of Bridgeton, New Jersey, at two dollars a copy.

The Unnatural History of South Jersey Lagoons

Kenneth W. Able

One of the most striking human influences along the coast of New Jersey was the development of lagoons for housing. These account for the transition of natural salt marshes into lagoon developments by dredging artificial channels and using the sediments from the dredging to create bulkheaded, home building sites with direct water access.[1] One prominent developer referred to the dredging of the marshes and the creation of lagoons during the mid-1900s as "manufacturing dirt" for home development.[2]

This process of lagoon development was initiated after WWII when there was increasing demand for housing and recreation-oriented development. It was further prompted by the construction of the Garden State Parkway and associated roadway enhancements in the 1950s. As a result, between 1940 and 1970, developers dredged and filled tens of thousands of acres of wetlands along the back bays such that one third of all coastal wetlands in New Jersey were impacted.[3]

The northern and southern portions of Barnegat Bay had the greatest area of lagoon development[4] and accompanying urbanization (Fig. 1).[5] This was evident on the back side of the barrier island and the mainland side in the northern portion of the bay. Development was less prominent on the back side of the southern portion of the barrier island, in large part because of the area preserved by Island Beach State Park. The areas less influenced by lagoon development are the Mullica River–Great Bay and Great Egg Harbor watersheds.

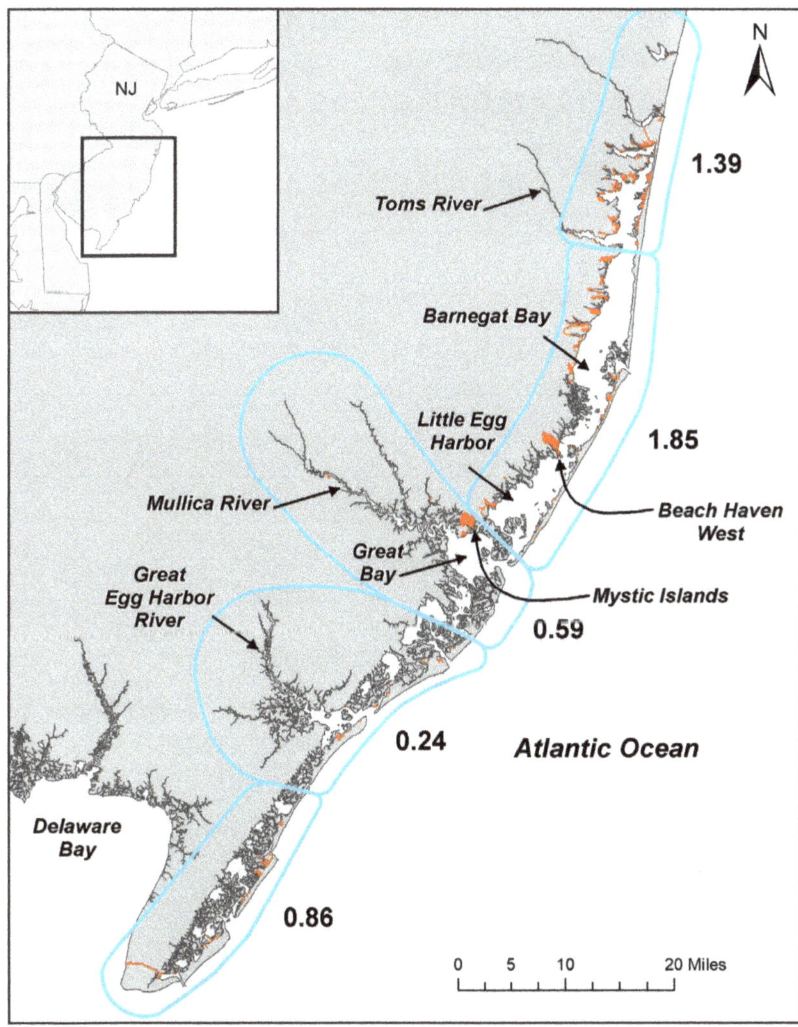

Figure 1. Distribution of lagoon developments (red) in coastal New Jersey based on NJDEP 2015 land use data. The values indicated are number of square miles of dredged lagoons by watershed area (outlined in blue).

Figure 2 (top). Early stages of lagoon development at Mystic Islands. See Fig. 1 for location. Figure 3 (bottom). Late stage of lagoon development at Mystic Islands. Original photos courtesy of Bob Greer from "Osbourne Island, Mystic Island, Little Egg Harbor, NJ" Facebook page.

However, one of the biggest lagoon developments was Mystic Islands in the upper portion of Great Bay (Fig. 1). Aerial photos of this development indicate the channels and associated filled areas that became housing sites (Fig. 2, 3) and eventually the community of Mystic Islands with about 4,500 homes.[6] A recent aerial image shows the current location of lagoon development in Mystic and Osbourne islands and the surrounding marshes that existed throughout the area before the dredging for lagoons (Fig. 4). Details of the construction of these lagoons are evident from one in Loveladies in Barnegat Bay where portions of the completed development are evident in the lower portion of the image (Fig. 5). Just above the developed portion is where former salt marsh has been dredged but portions of the marsh and some uplands are still evident because the development was not completed.

The most comprehensive evaluation of the ecological impacts of a lagoon development occurred in Barnegat Bay. Several small lagoons on the mainland side were evaluated and these efforts found that the lagoon waters were of poor quality due to weak circulation within the lagoons.[7] An even more detailed study was done for Beach Haven West, formerly known as the Remson Meadows salt marshes. This lagoon devel-

Figure 4. Image of Mystic Islands (right) and Osbourne Island (left) on March 7, 2019, from helicopter.

Figure 5. Image of lagoon development on Long Beach Island with developed (with houses) and undeveloped lagoons from helicopter on March 7, 2019. Photo courtesy of Jessica Valenti and K. W. Able.

opment was created in the same manner as other lagoon developments with the dredging of natural salt marshes to provide navigable channels and dredge spoil which was used to elevate the future home sites surrounding the channels (Fig. 6). This development covered 2.2 square miles with 104 dead end roads and channels (Fig. 7).

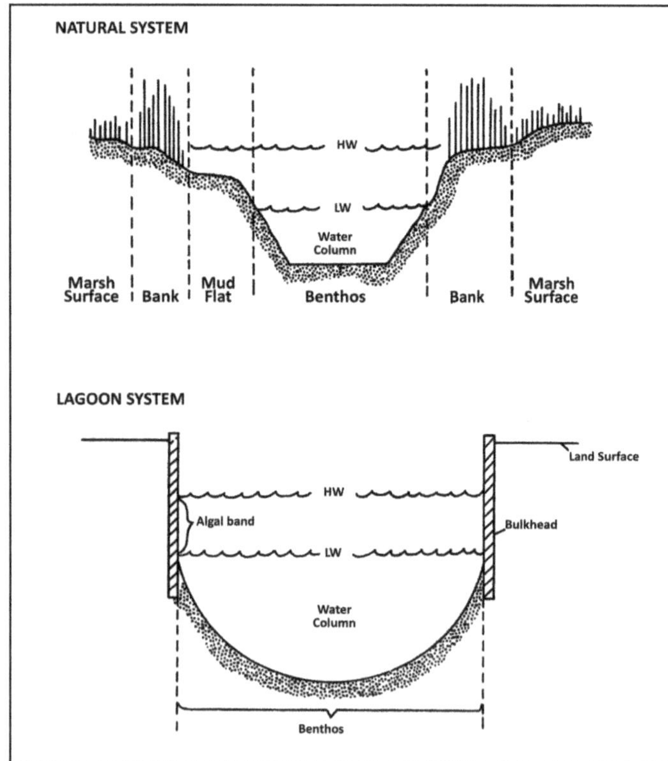

Figure 6. Diagrams of structure for representative salt marsh and lagoon systems (from Sugihara et al. 1979).

As an extensive study makes clear,[8] the productive marshes along Mill Creek that were the location of the Beach Haven West lagoon development have experienced extensive loss, infilling and development, resulting in the loss of vegetated marsh surface habitat and marsh pools and intertidal creeks. The lagoon system created less than optimal conditions including low dissolved oxygen (hypoxia/anoxia) in the summer. As a distinct example, the development apparently negatively influences recruitment of American eels in the Mill Creek watershed, in part because of the numerous dead-end channels with poor water quality.[9] A general summary of the ecological services provided by the adjacent natural marshes (Fig. 7) versus the Beach Haven West lagoon development indicate the negative effects of this development (Table 1). For example, salt marshes do provide numerous ecological services that lagoon developments, like Beach Haven West, do not provide to coastal landscapes. The important services provided by salt marshes include high production at the base of the food chain, buffer against storm damage, and refuge and foraging grounds for small fishes and crustaceans (i.e. nurseries). Many of these nurseries are especially critical to species in commercial and recreational fisheries.[10] In addition, there are other social and educational benefits of salt marshes including ecotourism, education, and aesthetics.[11]

There are numerous costs associated with maintaining these low-lying lagoon developments. One of the most frequent is the need to dredge because the slowing of water flow in the numerous dead-end channels in these developments causes sediments to accumulate and reduces the ability of boats to use the channels. This does not happen in natural salt marshes because they accumulate sediments and the marshes grow on top of these and in the process provide erosion control. The low-lying nature of lagoons makes them especially susceptible to sea level rise and the likelihood of the

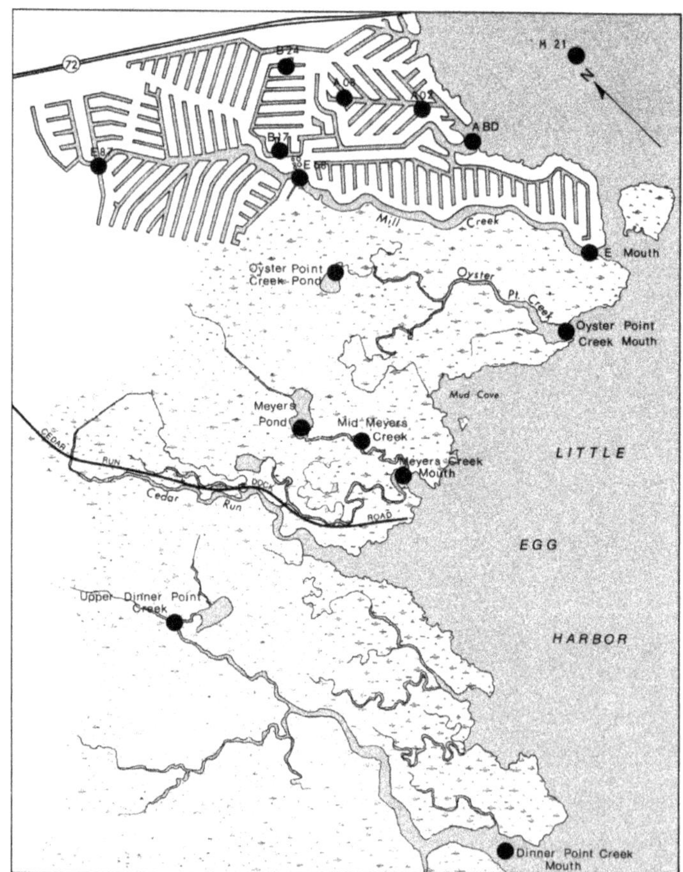

Figure 7. Map of Beach Haven West lagoon development and adjacent natural marsh areas used as reference sites for ecological comparisons: Oyster Point Creek, Meyers Creek, Cedar Run, Dinner Point Creek (from Sugihara et al. 1979). See Fig. 1 for location.

Ecological Services	Natural Marshes (General)	Beach Haven West
High production at base of food chain	+	-
Refuge and foraging grounds for small fishes and crustaceans	+	-
Feeding grounds for larger crabs and fishes during high water	+	-
Habitat for wildlife	+	-
Raw materials and human food	+	-
Water purification	+	-
Buffer against storm wave damage	+	-
Shoreline stabilization	+	-
Water quality	+	-
Biodiversity preservation	+	-
Carbon storage	+	-

Table 1. Summary of results from Beach Haven West relative to adjacent reference salt marsh based on observations in Sugihara et al. (1979). See Fig. 1 for general location and Fig. 6 for location of both. "+" indicates services available, "-" indicates services unavailable.

increasing frequency of major storms due to climate change.[12] The impacts of storms also provide evidence relevant to these comparisons. As an example, extensive flooding of Barnegat Bay during Superstorm Sandy[13] created damage to 4,000 of 4,500 houses in the lagoon development.[14] This flooding typically does not have extensive effects on natural marshes because they are inherently resilient to flooding.[15]

In other estuaries, similar dead-end canals have caused low dissolved oxygen conditions as well as increased production of hydrogen sulfide,[16] all of which can cause negative responses in many organisms.[17] The proliferation of these dead-end, artificial waterways is increasing on all continents,[18] and has resulted in the decline in habitat quality.

In summary, the findings from the Beach Haven West study and the resulting understanding of the value of salt marshes[19] contributed to New Jersey's Wetland Act of 1970. This legislation led to the demise of lagoon developments after it was passed.

About the Author

Ken Able is a Distinguished Professor Emeritus in the Department of Marine and Coastal Sciences and the former director of the Rutgers University Marine Field Station. His interests are diverse and include the relationship between the natural history and human history of estuaries and their watersheds.

Endnotes

1 G. H. Nieswand, C. W. Stillman and A. J. Esser, *Inventory of Estuarine Site Development Lagoon Systems: New Jersey Shore*, New Jersey Water Resources Research Institute (New Brunswick, NJ: Rutgers University, 1972). G. F. Walton, G. H. Nieswand, S. J. Toth, C. W. Stillman and J. R. Westman, *Evaluation of Estuarine Site Development Lagoons: Water Problems in an Urbanizing State*, New Jersey Water Resources Research Institute (New Brunswick, NJ: Rutgers University, 1976).

2 G. M. Gaul, *The Geography of Risk: Epic Storms, Rising Seas, and the Cost of America's Coasts* (New York: Sarah Crichton Books, 2019).

3 Gaul, *The Geography of Risk.*

4 M. J. Kennish, "Barnegat Bay-Little Egg Harbor Estuary and Watershed," *Journal of Coastal Research* no. 32 (Fall 2001): 243–73.

5 J. L. Valenti, T. M. Grothues and K. W. Able, "Estuarine Fish Communities Along a Spatial Urbanization Gradient," *Journal of Coastal Research* no. 78 (Fall 2017): 254–68.

6 Gaul, *The Geography of Risk.*

7 G. F. Walton et al., *Evaluation of Estuarine Site Development Lagoons.*

8 T. Sugihara, C. Yearsley, J. B. Durand and N. P. Psuty, *Comparison of Natural and Altered Estuarine Systems: Analysis and Field Data*, vol. 1 and 2, Rutgers University Center for Coastal and Environmental Studies. Publ. No. NJ/RU-DEP-119-79.

9 Kenneth W. Able, J. M. Smith and J. F. Caridad, "American Eel Supply to an Estuary and Its Tributaries: Spatial Variation in Barnegat Bay, New Jersey," *Northeastern Naturalist* 22, no. 1 (2015): 53–68.

10 Kenneth W. Able and M. P. Fahay, *Ecology of Estuarine*

Fishes: Temperate Waters of the Western North Atlantic (Baltimore, MD: Johns Hopkins University Press, 2010). Kenneth W. Able, *Beneath the Surface: Understanding Nature in the Mullica Valley Estuary* (New Brunswick, NJ: Rutgers University Press, 2020).
11 C. H. Peterson, K. W. Able, C. F. DeJong, M. F. Piehler, C. A. Simenstad and J. B. Zedler, "Practical Proxies for Tidal Marsh Ecosystem Services: Application to Injury and Restoration," *Advances in Marine Biology*, ed. D. W. Sims. vol. 54 (San Diego, CA: Academic Press, Elsevier Inc., 2008): 221–66.
12 Kenneth W. Able, *Beneath the Surface.*
13 J. L. Valenti, T. M. Grothues and K. W. Able, "Juvenile Fish Assemblage Recruitment Dynamics in a Mid-Atlantic Estuary: Before and After Hurricane Sandy," *Marine Ecology Progress Series* 641 (2020): 177–93.
14 Gaul, *The Geography of Risk.*
15 E. B. Barbier, S. D. Hacker, C. Kennedy, E. W. Koch, A. C. Stier and B. R. Silliman, "The Value of Estuarine and Coastal Ecosystem Services," *Ecological Monographs* 81, no. 2 (2011): 169–93.
16 G. W. Luther III, S. Ma, R. Trouwborst, B. Glazer, M. Blickley, R. W. Scarborough and M. G. Mensinger, "The Roles of Anoxia, H_2S, and Storm Events in Fish Kills of Dead-End Canals of Delaware Inland Bays," *Estuaries* 27, no. 3 (2004): 551–60.
17 T. Bagarinao, and I. Lantin-Olaguer, "The Sulfide Tolerance of Milkfish and Tilapia in Relation to Fish Kills in Farms and Natural Waters in the Philippines," *Hydrobiologia* no. 382 (1999): 137–50. T. Bagarinao and R. D. Vetter, "Sulfide Tolerance and Detoxification in Shallow-Water Marine Fishes, *Marine Biology* no. 103 (1989): 291–302. H. H. Seliger, J. A. Boggs and W. H. Biggley, "Catastrophic Anoxia in the Chesapeake Bay in 1984," *Science* no. 228 (1985): 70–73. H. Theede, "Comparative Studies on the Influence of Oxygen Deficiency and Hydrogen Sulphide on Marine Bottom Invertebrates," *Netherlands Journal of Sea Research* no. 7 (1973): 245–52.
18 N. J. Waltham and R. M. Connolly, "Global Extent and Distribution of Artificial, Residential Waterways in Estuaries," *Estuarine, Coastal and Shelf Science* no. 94 (2011): 192–97.
19 R. G. Lathrop Jr. and J. A. Bognar, "Habitat Loss and Alteration in the Barnegat Bay Region," *Journal of Coastal Research* no. 32 (2001): 212–28.

THE WASHINGTON HOTEL COLORED 6TH AND SIMPSON AVENUES OCEAN CITY, N. J.
EVERY ROOM AN OUTSIDE ROOM, WITH RUNNING WATER MEALS REFRESHMENTS
CHAS. BRYDSON, PROP. PHONE 591

In the days of Jim Crow and segregation, Atlantic City's Chicken Bone Beach became the most widely known location at the Jersey Shore where African Americans could enjoy time on the beach. Hotels designated for "colored" provided accommodations for those individuals and families spending more than just a day. Despite this location's fame, other Jersey beach towns offered hotels for people of color. Early in 1925, the Millville construction firm of Moore & Slade began building a hotel for William Thomas at Sixth Street and Simpson Avenue in Ocean City: "for colored folks exclusively and will accommodate from 65 to 70 guests. There is running water in every room and steam heat." The Thomas Hotel opened in June 1925 with a special event held under the auspices of the United Coolidge Club. In 1931, Thomas sold the facility to Charles Brydson, who renamed it the Washington Hotel. No listing for the hotel can be found in The Green Book the late 1940s. In August 1960, the Washington Hotel underwent an auction with Mrs. E. J. Benning buying the property, which she renamed the Benning Hotel. The 1962 Green Book has a listing for the Benning Hotel, but based on a review of historic aerial photographs, the building had disappeared from the corner of Sixth and Simpson sometime in 1963.

Warbirds Over the Pinelands

Horace A. Somes Jr.

The word "Warbirds" may conjure up images of vintage military aircraft or perhaps Native American bird totems with their spread wings, bald eagles symbolizing war and thunder. These may seem out of place over the rural Pinelands surrounding the Wading, Mullica, and Bass Rivers—whether it be the waterways and their watershed, or the so-named community of Wading River that extends from Turtle Creek Neck in Washington Township into the old Bridgeport area of Bass River Township. The skies have, however, witnessed an assorted mix of aircraft and military flights over the past century. Residents have both heard the "thunder" and seen the varied flight paths of jet aircraft approaching the nearby Warren Grove Target Range across the otherwise peaceful sky—or into the ground or water when an unfortunate accident occurs. Residents also may have viewed vintage planes overhead, en route to the Atlantic City airshow, or heard the loud engine of a modern "crop-duster" or biplane, as it "wages war" against pests in local cranberry bogs or is used by the State Forest Fire Service to attack wildfires in the Pineland forests. Knowledgeable bird-watchers also will spot the bald eagles that have returned to the rivers in recent decades, whether soaring over the waters and marshes, perching on riverside treetops, or nesting in the forest canopy where they now raise young each winter. The following provides some historical observations and anecdotes of the broader definition of the "warbirds" whose overhead presence extends back into the 1930s over this rural area of the Pinelands and coast.

Native American totem of bald eagle, *thunderbird.*

"Duck stamps" are required by the US Department of Interior for the hunting of migratory waterfowl under New Jersey Fish and Wildlife licensing regulations. A pair of vintage stamps from 1944 and 1945, issued at the end of the Second World War, appear to be affixed by their adhesive to an old hunting license. Closer examination, however, indicates that they were attached to an official identification card for an observer in the Aircraft Warning Service that existed from 1941 to 1944 for homeland protection during the height of World War II. Benjamin F. Cavileer had signed the front of the card. He was a local farmer from Lower Bank who had volunteered as a civilian "spotter." He probably served a post at the Lower Bank Landing, opposite today's River Road Clamhouse—which his cousin, Horace Cavileer, developed as a business establishment, taking advantage of the region's natural resources, as well as the geographic location on the Mullica River.

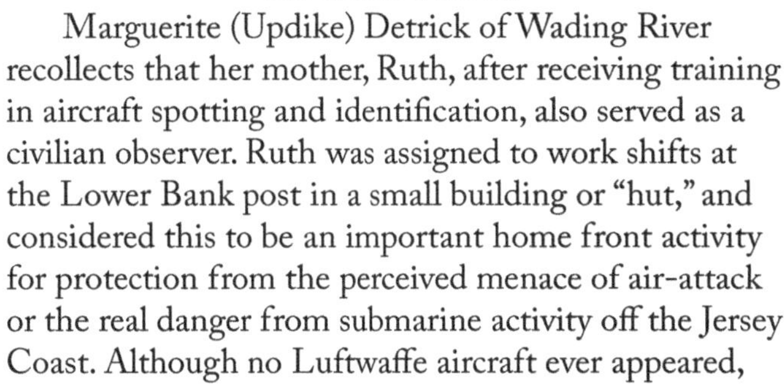

Marguerite (Updike) Detrick of Wading River recollects that her mother, Ruth, after receiving training in aircraft spotting and identification, also served as a civilian observer. Ruth was assigned to work shifts at the Lower Bank post in a small building or "hut," and considered this to be an important home front activity for protection from the perceived menace of air-attack or the real danger from submarine activity off the Jersey Coast. Although no Luftwaffe aircraft ever appeared, the sinkings by U-boats offshore did occur—and there was a risk of infiltrators being landed for sabotage or spying, as occurred elsewhere along the coast. Dorothy (McAnney) Somes of Wading River also recalled a lookout "cabin" at a promontory on Goldecker Road, overlooking the Wading River at the eastern end of the old Bridgeport bridge. She remembers, when she was a young resident, that this wartime "lookout" was supposedly for enemy submarines—although even "midget" vessels were a very improbable scenario on the narrow and winding rivers, as well as the shoals that extended through Great Bay to the ocean. Both the Lower Bank and Goldecker positions were, however, good observation points for overhead aircraft as well as activity on the waterways. Either river could conceivably have been a route for an infiltrator who chose not to land on a seaside beach, then under active military patrol mounted on horseback or trekking the miles of sandy strips. A military beach guard thwarted a group of saboteurs landing on Long Island after they came ashore from a U-boat. Local residents also proved invaluable in observing any potentially suspicious activities in their hometowns and along the waterways.

"Duck Stamps," or Migratory Waterfowl Hunting Endorsement, affixed to the front (above) and back (opposite page) of Benjamin F. Cavileer's Aircraft Spotter Identification card. Courtesy of Barbara L. Somes. Below: Aircraft Warning Service Pin. Courtesy of the Air Mobility Command Museum.

Before the outbreak of war for America, the dirigible Hindenburg was a harbinger of future events when it visited South Jersey airspace. On its final trip to Lakehurst Naval Air Station in May 1937, storm conditions forced a detour to the south along the coast past Manahawkin and Tuckerton before returning northward where it crashed in flames during landing, killing many on board and a member of the landing crew on the ground. Debate continues whether the airship's destruction was an accident, or intentional sabotage by someone opposed to the developing regime in Germany.

Horace Somes Sr. served as the forester for the Civilian Conservation Corps (CCC) camp at Bass River and recollected a long-distance view of the airship from the Little Egg Harbor area. A small photograph in the family collection depicts a small bright cylindrical object in the distant sky beyond a cow pasture; he later learned of the disaster. Two local residents, however, had a closer view of the airship as it passed overhead. Although air traffic associated with Atlantic City Airport and Joint Base McGuire-Dix-Lakehurst is now commonplace—as well as military flights into the Warren Grove Gunnery Range when scheduled—"lighter-than-air" craft were a noteworthy presence in South Jersey airspace in the middle of the twentieth century when the rigid airships were joined and then supplanted by the more-frequent blimps from the Naval Air Station at Lakehurst.

Steve Eichinger of Wading River recollects that his mother Martina and another family member observed the Hindenburg as it passed to the west of Wading River, then turned northbound for Lakehurst and its final destiny. A different, closer sighting occurred to the west at Lower Bank, where residents also observed its passage. Marguerite Detrick recalls that she and her mother had gone to Lower Bank to pick up her father, Jim Updike, after work at the Leek boat works. While they were there, the Hindenburg passed over Lower Bank and she vividly recollects a brief hovering, the swastika clearly visible on the tail. She felt a bit of curiosity, and perhaps awe, due to this Nazi emblem—although America was not yet in the war that was igniting across the oceans in Europe and Asia.

SPACE FOR PHOTO OR THUMB PRINT

Description of Observe

(To be filled in by Chief Observer

Signa

This pass may be revoked a. any ...

Observer or any authorized representative of the

Although the Lakehurst accident effectively ended the era of commercial dirigibles, the HINDENBURG was a precursor to the wartime history that would introduce military aircraft and their activities to the local airspace. Wartime need, and aviation technology, would bring blimps from Lakehurst to the Jersey shore for submarine patrols. On rare occasions today, such aircraft may return to the region in the form of smaller blimps for corporate advertising along the coast. When flying over Atlantic City, these single envelope, helium-filled airships may be seen at a distance and at altitude from the Mullica region.

World War II brought no warfare overhead to the Pinelands, although several local residents served in various overseas capacities, with some dying in service to their country. As evidenced by the Aircraft Observer identification card of Cavileer, local residents served in voluntary positions along the coast. The Jersey shore also hosted aviation bases that provided both military protection and training functions, including stations locally at Atlantic City and nearby at Wildwood and Millville. Training flights and practice missions utilized the rural airspace. In addition to the Warren Grove Gunnery Range, the wetlands between Ballanger Creek at the Ocean County boundary and the old New York Road in adjacent Bass River Township also featured a target range. Referred to as the outlying "Zable" Tract of Bass River State Forest, practice targeting in the tidal marshland deposited various ordnance in the muck soils near a peninsula of woods and the tributary named Worlds End Creek that flowed through the meadows into Ballanger Creek. Hay Road, from a section of Old Route 9, bisected the low elevation upland. This unpaved road was aptly named as it provided access to the extensive marshland containing salt hay (*Spartina patens*) that was historically harvested for livestock feed and bedding, as well as other past uses.

Steve Eichinger has a vivid recollection of this target range, where the pilots used the former Tuckerton wireless tower as an aiming point on Radio Road at what was then an elevation called Hickory Island. The tower had been erected to a height of several hundred feet prior to World War I by a German business for trans-Atlantic communications. When the United States entered the First World War, the government seized the radio tower and broadcast facilities and expelled the German nationals from the property. The tall structure remained as a local landmark until the mid 1950s when it was taken down. Shortly thereafter the adjacent land was developed as the Mystic Islands residential community. The massive concrete blocks that anchored the stabilizing cables for the tower remain in several nearby lagoons.

After passing over the tower, the pilots would align their aircraft for the approach to the old range by aim-

The HINDENBURG passes over the Manahawkin Bridge on the southbound leg of the storm detour from its scheduled landing at NAS Lakehurst. Courtesy of the Tuckerton Historical Society, Adams family collection.

ing at a large wooden arrow constructed in the marsh near Ballanger Creek. The target was a circular area of marsh approximately 100 feet in diameter. Three small buildings housed Naval personnel who acted as spotters to monitor the flights and the accuracy of the targeting. The weapons used at the range included the dropping of small practice bombs, as well as the firing of wing-mounted air-to-ground rockets. One building position monitored altitude and angle of approach, while the other two provided cross-readings on the impacts in the target area. Current aerial photography depicts features in the marsh at the now-overgrown Bombing Range Road including former ditches and embankments that served to identify the range and target for the pilots.

"Locals" soon discovered that the facility was not regularly staffed or secured and could be a source of scrap metal with value. Freezing winter weather could harden the marsh, causing the ordnance to stay on the surface or skip away from the impact target, making the bombs and rockets accessible. Care had to be taken as the ordnance might include explosive charges to mark the impact location for the spotters on the ground as well as the pilots passing overhead.

Subsequent development of the nearby marsh-land as Mystic Islands, as well as later excavations and re-development, has unearthed old munitions requiring proper disposal. Horace Somes Sr., Wading River, recollected seeing an old torpedo in a creek bottom while duck hunting after the war with Milton Kauflin from New Gretna. His son Frank later worked for the Burlington County Mosquito Commission. While ditching with machinery for marsh drainage near Ballanger, workmen encountered the remnants of old air-to-ground rockets.

Training flights unfortunately resulted in air-to-ground mishaps for aircraft as recalled by Steve Eichinger, Wading River, whose relatives had previously witnessed the Hindenburg flight. On one occasion, while on the dock at Chips Folly resort at the Broad Place on the river, he witnessed an explosion in the woods to the northeast of the old New Gretna-Chatsworth Road (now County Route 679). His father had been working at the cranberry bogs on Ives Branch, at what is now Timberline Lake, and observed a plane crash into the nearby forest. A pilot, presumably on a military training mission, crashed his plane between Ives Branch and Tub Mill Branch. They later traveled to the site at a promontory called Clay Hill, where they found scattered debris and the aftermath of a small brushfire resulting from the crash. The pilot reportedly died in the mishap.

On another occasion, Steve had gone with his aunt Alice Weber on one of their frequent boating trips for either fish or snapping turtles. Downriver between Merrygold and the Mullica River, they had observed the tail or wing of an aircraft protruding from the water near the riverbank. This was one of two planes that had crashed in the area of Swan Bay, the other landing in the tide marsh west of Turtle Creek. The military had subsequently reinforced the small bridge over Billys Creek at the end of Turtle Creek Road, leading to a small landing used by fishermen, trappers, hunters, and salt-hay harvesters. This allowed vehicular access to recover that plane from the marsh. Today, to the east of Swan Bay, where low tide had formerly exposed the second plane, a lack of underwater remnants suggests that it too has been recovered. Another military plane crashed to the east of the Bass River and to the west of the fire tower on Greenbush Road. The impact was reportedly severe, and the motor deeply buried into the forest. The CCC, Civilian Conservation Corps, whose camp was established on Greenbush near Stage Road in the mid-1930s, erected the metal lookout tower for the State Forest Fire Service, which also could have provided a military service when the Army occupied the CCC facilities after war broke out.

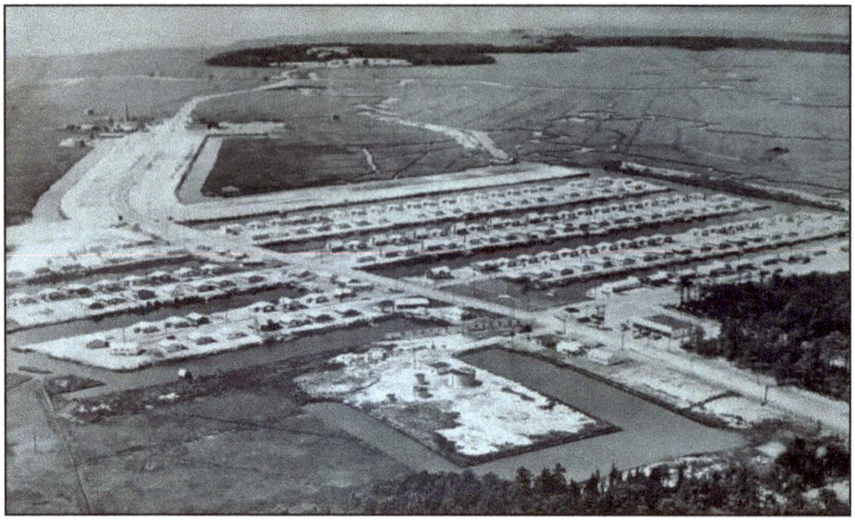

Mystic Island, shown above during its initial development in the 1960s, once was the site of the massive Tuckerton wireless tower, used by pilots as a landmark during target practice flights. Photograph courtesy of the Tuckerton Historical Society.

Mishaps by military operations and aircraft were not limited to the war years. In 1971, a fighter-bomber mission to the Warren Grove Range, piloted by Major William F. Dimas Jr., resulted in a crash into the Bear Swamp Hill Fire Tower of the New Jersey Forest Fire Service in Penn State Forest near Lake Oswego on the Wading River, East Branch. Horace Somes Sr. was trapping for muskrats at the time along the Wading River and observed the distant smoke plume from the crash. Although the fire observer was fortunately off-duty for the winter, the pilot was an unfortunate fatality. After crashing through a lower landing of the tower stairs and nearby tree trunks, the plane impacted the top of the promontory before the remnants glided across the adjacent pineland to the east. Wing parts broke off as the plane passed through additional treetops, with the explosion scorching a swath of the forest. The landing gear also broke off as the plane entered the cedar swamp and both wheels and struts apparently remain hidden in the woods today. Fortunately, the resulting fire did not spread far from the crash explosion due to the winter conditions. Research of Air Force records by James Gilbert, Tuckerton, has documented the three-quarter-mile-long crash path as well as a hill-top view of the tower wreckage. The remnant fuselage gouged through the nearby cedar of Bear Swamp before stopping. The military later recovered the fuselage. Remains of the heavy engines were mapped as having continued through the forest toward Sim Place, coming to rest before reaching Lake Oswego Road. For several years, the notch cut in the tree canopy on the hilltop could be viewed from the neighboring tower on Apple Pie Hill.

Remnants of the landing gear found west of Bear Swamp, following the 1971 crash that took the life of Major William F. Dimas Jr.

Bear Swamp Hill fire tower prior to its 1971 collapse resulting from the damage sustained in a fatal airplane crash. This and all unattributed images appear courtesy of the author.

Both Bear Swamp Hill and nearby Spring Hill, located at the northeast boundary of the State Forest, offer broad vistas of the green expanse of Pinelands in the core of the "Barrens." The forest, however, also provides the fuel for wildfires within this fire-impacted ecosystem—whether ignited in modern times by people accidentally, carelessly, or intentionally, or prehistorically by lightning or Native Americans. Both Penn Forest and Warren Grove Range are associated with unique areas of dwarfed pines that have been referred to as the West (or Upper) and East (or Lower) Plains for centuries. Both to reduce the accumulation of forest fuels as well as maintain fire as an ecosystem element, the state on Penn and the military at Warren Grove use the controlled application of fire under prescribed conditions. However, no fire tower remains at Bear Swamp to provide a lookout over the forest vista, which is now over-watched by other posts at Bass River, Apple Pie Hill, and Cedar Bridge. Spotting towers at the nearby Warren Grove Range also contribute to fire detection in this region, as well as the monitoring of weather conditions and fire behavior during burns to reduce fire hazards in the forests around the targets for the variety of munitions used in training exercises. Due to the remoteness, restricted utility service, and the increasing prevalence of vandalism and misuse of such Pinelands, it was deemed not cost-effective to rebuild the tower at Bear Swamp Hill—a recognized and mapped topographic feature dating back to the mid-nineteenth century.

Coincidentally, the State Forests in the area had been the sites of camps for the CCC during the Great Depression of the 1930s. These camps served as the bases for Park development at Bass River, Penn, and Green Bank, where a tree nursery also operated to produce seedlings for landscaping, as well as reforestation due to the catastrophic wildfires that historically spread throughout the Pine Barrens. The CCC crews also rebuilt the fire lookout towers at Bass River and Bear Swamp Hill—although the original 1921 wooden structure at Penn experienced wildfire damage. The Bear Swamp tower later underwent modernization with a used surplus steel structure, which the Forest Fire Service relocated from Monmouth County. With the onset of World War II, the federal government disbanded CCC camps, but Army units occupied the facilities at Bass River and Green Bank.

Interestingly, the local history of the State Park Service indicates that the United States Army conducted a large-scale maneuver in May 1941 that involved the three local parks and CCC facilities. As the military prepared for anticipated warfare, a simulated invasion along the coast involved neighboring states as the aggressor "Red land." A force of 16,000 troops

Aviation map of the region: The Mullica River forms the marked boundary between Atlantic and Burlington Counties. Clockwise from the Mullica are the Wading River, visible east of Wharton State Forest, and the Bass River, faintly visible running south from Bass River State Forest to its confluence with the Mullica, where the three counties of Atlantic, Burlington, and Ocean meet. Due north from Bass River State Forest is the U. S. Navy Reservation, with Penn State Forest to its northwest and Warren Grove Range to its northeast. Ballanger Creek and Mystic Island are located within the small shaded region, north of Great Bay, where the rivers meet the Atlantic Ocean. (Defense Mapping Agency Hydrographic/Topographic Center)

were mobilized to defend the "Blue land" and deployed on foot and in trucks through the Pinelands to Penn, Bass River, and Green Bank. Several infantry regiments, artillery, engineers, signal corps, and medical units were stationed at Lake Oswego, Green Bank, and north of Bass River near Munion Field. Although no aviation support is recorded, the troops, weapons, and tents apparently needed little camouflage from the sky as the dust from the sand roads and two-thousand trucks hung in the air day and night.

Air power, however, would develop and become a major component of the military during both the Second World War and the subsequent "Cold War." In addition to the operational air bases at nearby McGuire, Lakehurst, and Atlantic City, training was necessary and the then-remote Pine Barrens furnished unimpeded airspace. The United States Navy, based at the Atlantic City airport in Pomona, developed the training and research facility at Warren Grove. The training facility continues to this day between Penn and Bass River parks as a target range of the New Jersey National Guard. Although the tidal marsh target area at Ballanger Creek was abandoned, Coyle Field, once used for military training to the north of Penn on the West Plain, is now the aviation center of the Forest Fire Service that utilizes both rotary helicopter and fixed-wing planes for air-attack on wildfires and the necessary aerial support for suppression operations.

Decades later, an air crash in the summer of 1986 resulted in a major wildfire after an F-4 fighter-bomber attempted to gain altitude following a pass over the Warren Grove Range. As it flew across Bear Swamp in

New Jersey Forest Fire Service contracted air tanker, stationed at Coyle Field Aviation Base.

Penn State Forest, an engine failure resulted in a crash into the West Plains of the Warren Grove Recreation Area, which is another outlying tract of Bass River State Forest. Both pilots were fortunately able to eject before the plane made a near-vertical impact in the Pinelands. The impact gouged a deep crater near the intersection of Sooy Road, which passes the old tower site, and Long Causeway, which crosses the West Plains. The explosion ignited a wildfire of approximately one hundred acres before it was controlled by the Forest Fire Service, preventing a larger conflagration. The military detailed an armed squad to provide overnight security and the Forest Fire Service also posted a patrol unit to ensure that the fire remained within the control lines. The guards deployed to picket posts around the road intersection, and set up their guard sites that included small campfires for the overnight hours. The local district fire warden, who was patrolling the area, dutifully instructed that the campfires be extinguished as the fire weather and dry forest was hazardous, and a campfire ban had been imposed in the Pinelands. The heavily-armed guards respectfully complied and continued their overnight duties with their flashlights and weapons—but no campfires.

Aerial view of the Warren Grove Bombing Range.

A subsequent low-flight approach to the range did have a very-localized but minor impact on the "home front." In the past, planes using the range included a small but powerful bomber—the F111 or "Aardvark." Also referred to as the "Pig," its powerful engines could vibrate the ground

A retired A-7 Corsair rests in the field at Warren Grove Range. In the distance the spotting tower is visible above the tree line.

at low altitude. On one low pass over Turtle Creek Neck, it was said that "someone had chain-sawed" an upstairs bedroom ceiling in the old McAnney homestead on the Somes's farm. Inspection by the homeowner revealed that the old drywall ceiling had fallen as a possible coincidence of the very-old mortar and the vibrations from the very low and loud jet engines. No injury or other damage had occurred—other than the clean-up mess for mom. The family became good spotters for the different types of planes that flew over the area and into the range. A model collection of aircraft visiting the range was hung from the stronger ceiling in a downstairs room, and ranged from attack planes (e.g., A4, F4, F6, A10) to helicopters used for observation, troop transportation, and air support. For the spotters of the war years, identification cards with aircraft silhouettes and descriptions would have been supplemented with similarly scaled models to indicate the different aircraft—both friend and foe. While spotters for the First Interceptor Command of the northeast coast would have trained for German aircraft, spotters on the west coast would have also contended with the "balloon bombs" that sailed the prevailing wind patterns from Japan to the states of the Northwest Pacific.

A "near-miss" occurred in January 2002 when a F-16 Fighting Falcon crashed in Bass River State Forest to the east of Lake Absegami Recreation Area. Fortunately, due to the winter month, park visitors and campers were absent. The pilot also was fortunate, bailing out into the nearby Pinelands. The ground impact was a short distance to the west of the Garden State Parkway, where the Forest Fire Service initially gained access to the site and multiple federal, state, and local agencies responded. As the resources were demobilizing, two deer hunters arrived at the park office and reported that they had been in the woods to the east of the Parkway near Munion Field Road. They indicated that several pieces of debris had landed through the trees—which would have required pieces of wreckage to have continued from the crash site across both the south and north bound lanes of the heavily traveled highway. Although some debris had been found on the west shoulder of the roadway, it was fortunate that none had struck any of the passing cars, trucks, and buses.

It also was fortunate that neither the F-16 nor a prior crash of an A-10 Warthog resulted in Pineland wildfires. To the north of the State Forest, the A-10 went down in the Stafford Forge Wildlife Management Area, west of the Shotgun Target Range and County Route 539, but remote from people and homes. The location, however, was in the hazardous forest fuels at the southeastern end of the East Plains of dwarf pines. Subsequent expansion of the cooperative program of prescribed burning included this area with other Pinelands of the Wildlife Area, State Forest, and Warren Grove Range for both the mitigation of wildfire hazards and management of the fire-adapted ecosystem of the Pine Barrens.

The military aircraft varied over time, with evolving avionics and changes in military units utilizing the range. The F-4 Phantom of the Vietnam War era was a frequent visitor until retired from active service. Like the F-111, its twin engines were powerful and loud—but its weaponry varied from guns, to rockets, and bombs. For several seasons, Barbara Somes, Wading River, supervised farm laborers where she worked as foreman at the Wading River Cranberry Bogs. A few of those seasons involved the work of recent emigrants from Southeast Asia, and they brought with them agricultural capabilities and work traits from their homelands of Vietnam or Cambodia. They worked industriously after morning and noon meals, which might have included native plants and animals

BDU (Bomb Dummy Unit) found on Stafford Forge Wildlife Management Area. BDUs are often used by the Air Force in place of live munitions.

Smoke column from a prescribed burning on Warren Grove Range. Viewed from Route 679 at Timberline Lake, Bass River Township, 1999.

in the cuisine. The diked and ditched bogs also had a somewhat-similar appearance to the rice paddies of Southeast Asia. On one occasion, a Phantom jet swooped in low over a sandy ridge to the west. As the jet continued its flight path to "attack" targets on the range, it was found that the work crew had taken cover off the diked roadways, in the bogs and ditches. It took a few minutes for everyone to be accounted for and re-organized to continue the harvest work.

Low-level training operations employed a variety of ordnance containing incendiary elements capable of causing forest fires beyond a crash landing. This became increasingly apparent in the decades following the 1960s, as the range expanded both its activities and facilities for military aerial training that was somewhat unique to the mid-Atlantic region. Practice bombs, referred to as BDU's ("bomb dummy units"), could have a "spotter charge" to mark their impact proximity to the intended target. This equivalent to a super-sized shotgun shell could ignite the leaf litter when the bomb penetrated the forest floor. Rocket motors were similar to civilian fireworks, which also cause July 4th fires when used illegally. "Tracer" ammunition bullets, by definition and construction, include pyrotechnic elements that may ignite forest fuels under dry weather conditions. Protective flares also could be ejected to simulate the deflection of anti-aircraft fire from the ground. However, flares dropped from aircraft at low altitude over the flammable East Plains could become incendiary objects when weather creates hazardous conditions in the Pineland forest. Although the range property consists of several thousand acres, high airspeeds and low altitudes for ordnance release could result in impacts and fire ignitions in adjacent State Forest and Wildlife areas.

Silhouetted A-10 Warthogs fly in formation after a training mission at Willow Grove Range.

Ultimately, an accidental fire that originated from range operations in 2007 posed a serious and direct threat to nearby communities and disrupted regional traffic due to smoke and/or fire impacts upon major highways. Restriction of ordnance types and hazard reduction on both range and adjacent state lands has currently diminished this risk. Today, a large smoke column on the horizon from the Wading River will most likely be a wintertime controlled burn for hazard reduction on state or private forest lands, or at the Warren Grove Range, where the Forest Fire Service cooperates with military personnel.

A vintage B-24 Liberator is displayed on the tarmac of NAS Wildwood Aviation Museum, following a "fly-in" to Cape May Airport's AirFest 2011.

Today, the skies over the Mullica, Wading, and Bass rivers are most noticeably crisscrossed by modern "warbirds" of the Country's military, as training progresses at the Warren Grove Range. Administered through the 177th Fighter Wing of the New Jersey Air National Guard at Atlantic City Airport, the range has undergone much transformation since the inception of activities in the 1940s in the core of the Pinelands. The nicknames for aircraft of recent decades have ranged from the benign Aardvark (F-111) to the warlike Skyhawk (A-4), Phantom (F-4), and Fighting Falcon (F-16), with the dichotomous A-10 straddling both sides—ubiquitously known as the Warthog, yet at times referred to by its official nickname, the Thunderbolt. Less frequently and at distant altitude, historic warbirds may come into view as they participate in annual airshows, which have been held on the Atlantic City beach and the NAS Wildwood Aviation Museum at Cape May County Airport for some years. In static display on the tarmac, there is the opportunity to get up close and personal with aircraft that contributed to the victory in World War II.

Today, the skies are also frequented by the bald eagle, which also could have been seen as a thunderbird by the Native Americans who originally crisscrossed the Pinelands on their trails. This totem could symbolize thunder as well as war. Through environmental protection efforts, this national emblem has returned to the region with nesting along the rivers and regular perching in advantageous lookout trees for spotting game and resting between flights. Care must be taken to not mistake the eagles for buzzards that are more prevalent but have distinctively different flight patterns and profiles. An experienced bird watcher can discern the difference between the established turkey vulture and the newly arrived black vulture. During the winter influx of migrants, careful discrimination may be needed as the larger golden eagle may be in the area to benefit from the waterway resources and riverside perching. They might be considered as spotters to the overland, overwater, and underwater, as they search for food for themselves and nest hatchlings of one or more young. Recent successful nesting and population improvement documents the success of their hunting for underwater fish, overwater waterfowl, and in-water turtles and muskrats.

An experienced aircraft "spotter" also can discriminate between the modern "warbirds," the civilian traffic into nearby Atlantic City Airport, or more distant military flights into Joint Base McGuire-Lakehurst-Dix. It may now be considered a pastime to make these distinctions: military versus civilian, F16 vs. F18 vs. A10, or crop-duster vs. forestry air tanker. As this article has stated, in the recent past there were local civilian volunteer "spotters" along the rivers on the lookout for the threat of wartime enemies, either in the air or on the water. They received training and served work shifts for the Aircraft Warning Service. Although not tested by attack from the air or invasion from the sea, they were a part of the country's preparedness—as are today's aviators who train and practice in the "warbirds" over today's Pinelands.

Bald Eagle *"thunderbirds"* in Wading River.

The Wading River upstream of the highway bridge at Old Bridgeport—now the community of Wading River, circa 1960s. Courtesy of Steve Eichinger.

About the Author

Horace A. Somes Jr., a lifelong resident of the coastal New Jersey Pinelands, spent his career working for the New Jersey Forest Fire Service, as an environmental consultant, and in various NJDEP positions. Though retired, he is currently a member of the Tuckerton Historical Society and a business partner—with his brother Frank—for Wading River Christmas Tree Farm.

The author would like to recognize the important contributions of Steve Eichinger, Brian Detrick, and James Gilbert to this article.

References

The author consulted the following materials while conducting research for this work.

Air National Guard. USAF Accident/Incident Report. Lewis W. Weber. Air Force form 711b #71-1-16-2. 1971. (Courtesy of USAF archival research by James Gilbert – Little Egg Harbor.)

"Aircraft Warning Service." *Wikipedia, The Free Encyclopedia.* https://en.wikipedia.org/wiki/Aircraft_Warning_Service.

Clark, George. "Air National Guard Jet Crash: 2 Injured in bailout over Pines." *Courier Post* (Camden, NJ), June 19, 1986. A1-4.

Galluzzo, John J. *Millville Army Air Field: America's First Defense Airport.* Charleston, SC: Arcadia Publishing, 2011.

Gordon, Jerry. "A Look Back at the History of Naval Air Station Atlantic City." *Press of Atlantic City*, July 2, 2018. https://pressofatlanticcity.com/history/a-look-back-at-the-history-of- naval-air-station-atlantic-city/article_1da25560-889c-51a2-a044-c1293d05d5c7.html.

"Hindenburg disaster." *Wikipedia, The Free Encyclopedia.* https://en.wikipedia.org/wiki/Hindenburg_disaster.

Mooney, Michael M. *The Hindenburg*. New York: Dodd, Mead, 1972.

NJ Department of Environmental Protection. Penn SF History Final (NJ, 2020). https://www.state.nj.us/dep/parksandforests/parks/docs/penn_sf_history.pdf.

"Pilot Safe After Fighter Jet Crashes in Woods." *New York Times*, January 11, 2002. B5.

Porcelli, Richard V. *Naval Air Station Atlantic City.* Charleston, SC: Arcadia Publishing, 2012.

RCH. "Warren Grove Bombing Range." virtualglobetrotting. https://virtualglobetrotting.com/map/warren-grove-bombing-range/view/google/.

Salvatore, Joseph E., and Joan Berkley. *Naval Air Station Wildwood.* Charleston, SC: Arcadia, 2009.

Thompson, Robert V. Sabers. *Hogs and Thuds: The Diary of a Part Time Cold War Fighter Pilot.* Bloomington, IN: AuthorHouse, 2003.

U.S. Air Force. "Warren Grove Range." Readiness and Environmental Protection Integration. United States Department of Defense. https://www.repi.mil/Portals/44/Documents/Buffer_Fact_Sheets/Air%20Force/WarrenGroveRange.pdf.

"Warren Grove: Flares Caused Forest Fire." *New York Times*, July 27, 2007. https://www.nytimes.com/2007/07/27/nyregion/27mbrfs-fire.html#:~:text=A%20military%20report%20has%20concluded,the%20Air%20Force%20announced%20yesterday.

"Warren Grove Gunnery Range." GlobalSecurity.org. https://www.globalsecurity.org/military/facility/warren-grove-r.htm.

The Still Brothers trilogy. Chronicling the extraordinary lives of Peter, James and William Still, children of Levin and Charity during the nineteenth century. Published by SJCHC and now available at Second Times Books, Mount Laurel, and Amazon.

Selections from the Noyes Decoy Collection

With captions by Gary Giberson

One gross of bluebill decoys (144) in the yard of Fred and Ethel Noyes at the Franklin Inn, Port Republic, New Jersey. Purchased from the Mud City Gun Club in Manahawkin, some of these decoys, true hunting lures, remain in the Noyes collection. When you shake them, shot rattles inside a few of them.

Decoy carving is a craft of long-standing in South Jersey. At their best, decoys capture the likeness and deportment of the waterfowl they emulate, for they have utilitarian origins: they needed to mimic live birds. Today decoys are considered examples of folk art, each carefully and uniquely crafted. They are specimens of a long-established and deeply rooted American tradition.

Before the arrival of European settlers, Native Americans created waterfowl decoys from reeds. These early decoys were intended to lure game into range. European settlers followed suit, but turned to carving decoys from local cedar. Hunters and sportsmen visiting the Jersey Shore in the late 1800s and early 1900s sought field guides who offered not only the best hunting locations, but also the most realistic decoys sourced from local carvers. Today, while some decoys are still fashioned and used in the hunt, many are carved for display alone. South Jersey has an especially rich carving heritage, given the long-standing baymen's lifestyle. Skilled carvers dot the map, offering their skills for collectors and hunters alike.

This brief selection brings this utilitarian art to light, featuring decoys collected by Fred Noyes Jr. for South Jersey's Noyes Museum of Art. Gary Giberson, who aided in the purchase of many of these decoys, describes each—Giberson is himself an expert carver. We hope his descriptions, with accompanying photographs, bring to life the spirit of each decoy, both in service and art.

Sarah E. Augustine

The following captions are edited versions of comments made by Gary Giberson on Armistice Day 2018, when Stockton students Claire Riley and Shannon Stolz visited Giberson, who selected the decoys and described interesting details.

Hudsonian Wimbrell Curlew (previous page)
The shorter bill of this Curlew decoy marks it as none other than a Wimbrell, a decoy carved by Harry Boice out of Absecon. A curlew is a bigger bird, which we can see by the body that is longer than most. Curlews vary by the length of their bill, long versus short, and this decoy is an example of a short-billed Curlew. At the Tuckerton Seaport sits a long-bill Curlew on loan from the Noyes collection that is one of a kind, the only decoy of its nature made. When Fred Noyes bought that long-bill, I drooled over it. I put it on posters and everything.

Green Wing Teal (this page)
This is a little Green Wing Teal. It is smaller than the average decoy at only 9½ inches long whereas most decoys are twelve or fourteen inches. It is a two-piece decoy with recessed lead in the bottom and has the Seabrook brand meaning that Bobby Seabrook, of Absecon, carved this decoy. Teal fly a little earlier in the season than the Black Ducks and the Mallards, following the Atlantic flyway and arriving in our area about two weeks before the other species. Decoys of the species are quite common. This was carved in 1979.

Red Head (this page)
This decoy is a Red Head. This species' decoys are unique to Manahawkin Bay in New Jersey because the Red Heads would fly into the bay with Canvasbacks. When you see something like this, you know it's from north of us, like Manahawkin and Tuckerton. We never got any Red Heads or Canvasbacks in Great Bay. The maker of this decoy is unknown. It was carved around 1900, and is made unique by the half-section of the tail which the carver just cut off, allowing the tail area to just go back a little further.

Red Breasted Merganser (next page top)
Joel Salmons was copying the master with his four-feather cuts, leaving this decoy from Tuckerton, New Jersey, to appear very Harry Shourds-like. The Red Breasted Merganser was thought by some to be not fit to eat—they were diving ducks that ate small fish, giving them an overwhelmingly fishy taste. However, others favored the taste of Mergansers in their stock pots. "What are you shooting that for?" someone would say, "It ain't fit to eat." The answer was yes, they were: the breast, leg and thigh meats were all utilized to make a tasty fish chowder with no fish bones.

Jersey Brant (next page bottom)
This 1915 Jersey Brant is special because "it's a Horner." Renowned carver Roley Horner from Mayetta, New Jersey, is considered by many to be New Jersey's best decoy maker. This Jersey Brant a large bird is almost eighteen inches long, which is bigger than the average decoy, and made from readily-available Atlantic White Cedar, which is an excellent carving material. Atlantic White Cedar is cut down in winter when the sap is down into the root system allowing the tree to get through the winter. This prevents thick, crystallized summer-time sap from dulling the carving tools. I cut Cedar down during Christmastime by lifting the butt of the tree to keep moisture from getting in. When I come back to get it and drag it out in April, I have the best wood in the world.

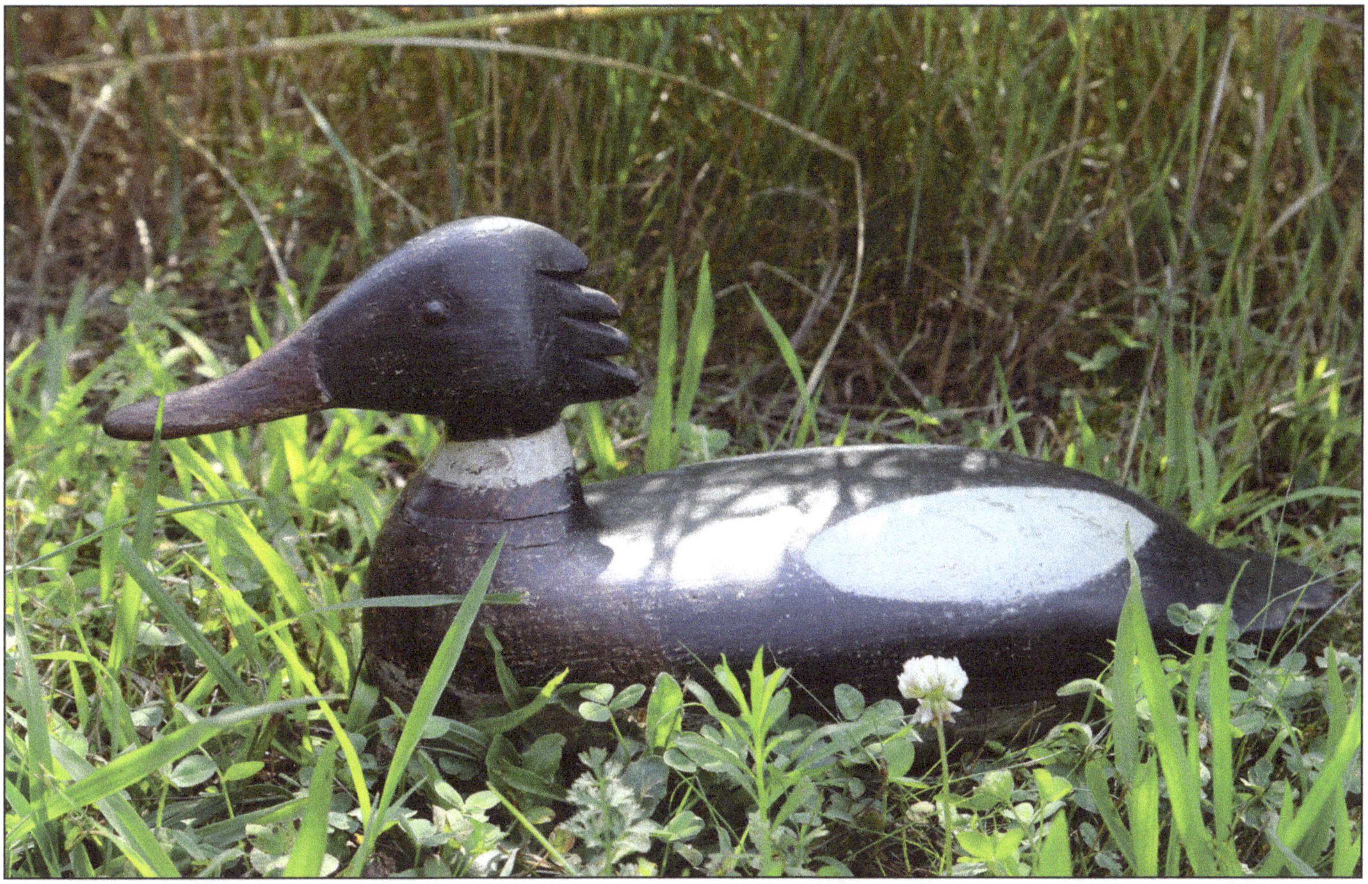

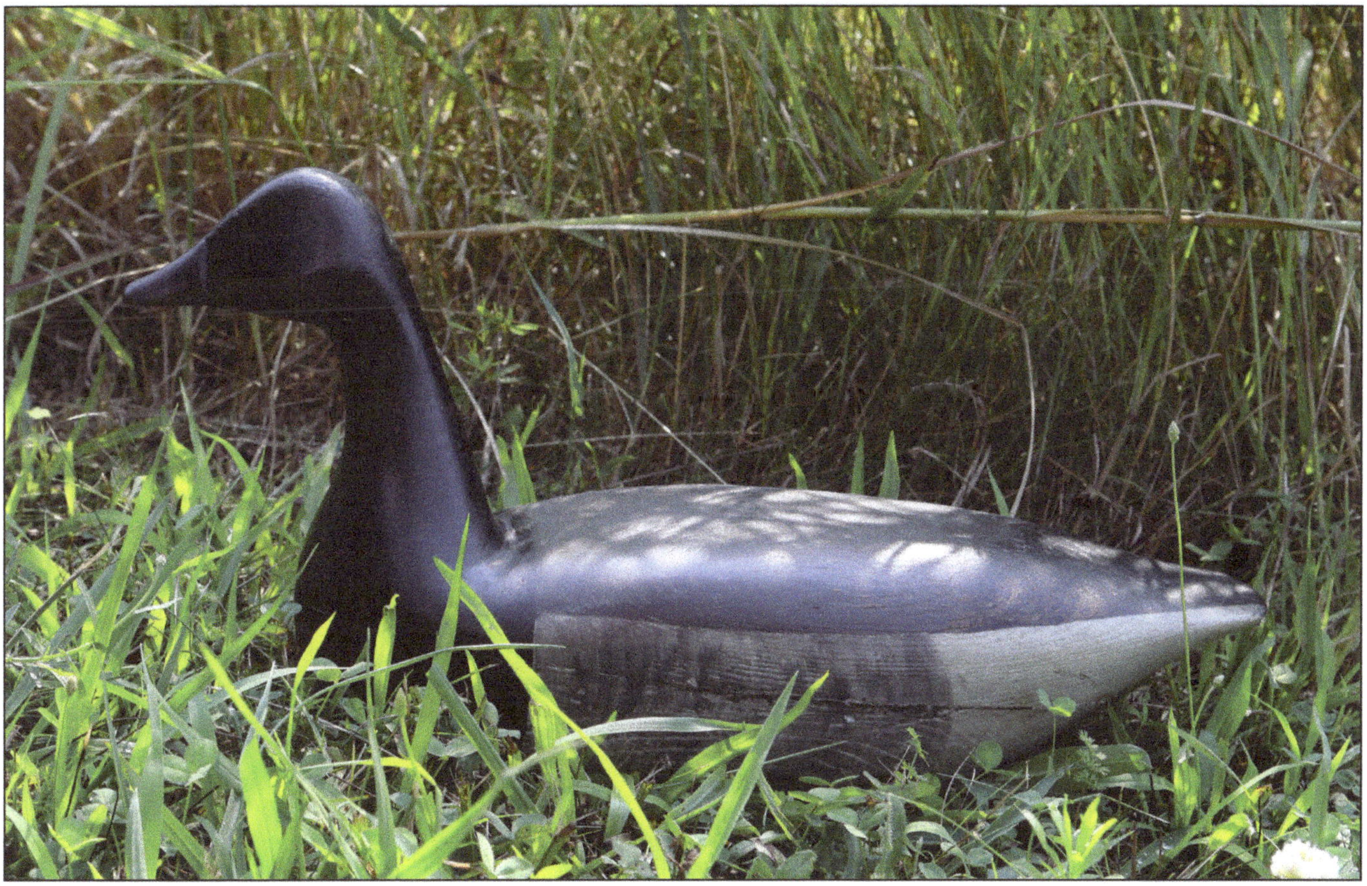

Brant (this page)

This is an decoy of a Brant, which is a small goose with a real short bill and real long neck. It is beautifully restored, but the identity of the carver is controversial. Both Liberty Price and Joe King have been named. I think it was carved by Liberty Price. It is one of the most beautiful New Jersey decoys that was ever made. I love this decoy. I carved many necks for Brant decoys; they are made with a cocked head, mimicking the Brant's undulating neck as it swims.

Jersey Pintail (next page top)

This Pintail decoy was made by an unknown New Jersey carver from the Maurice River area. Dated around 1928, it is unusual in Fred Noyes' collection as Pintails are not common in this area. This sixteen-inch, two-piece decoy is hollow and hand-painted. Notice the greens, blacks and whites used in painting this decoy. Ducks must have unbelievable color recognition because if they didn't, Pintails wouldn't flock to decoys like this.

Crow (next page bottom)

This crow decoy poses the question: who would shoot crows? The answer is "anybody." Because the crow is an enemy to the farmer. He eats the corn; he eats the seedlings. If not stopped, crows will damage and destroy a field. To be rid of the crop-eating crow, farmers would put up owl decoys—the crow hates the owl. They are mortal enemies. Or they would use crow decoys to attract the bird, and mimic the crow emergency call to alert them. Sometimes farmers would dip their corn kernels or whatever they were growing into a solution of tar and coal oil. That did not stop germination, but crows would pull one or two and find that they couldn't eat them and avoid that field. Between their language skills and their ability to remember bad-tasting kernels, I argue that crows are one of the smartest creatures in the world.

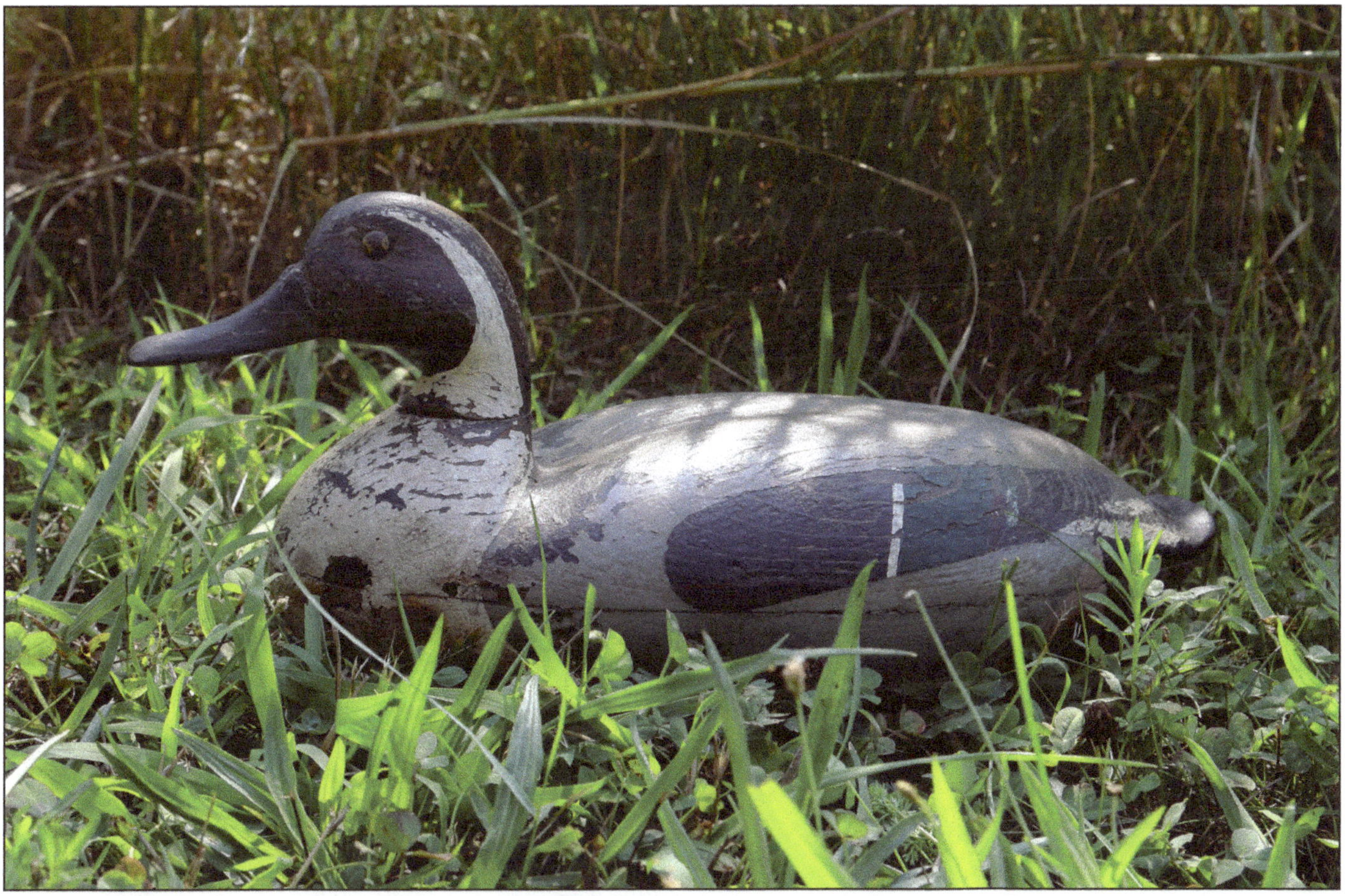

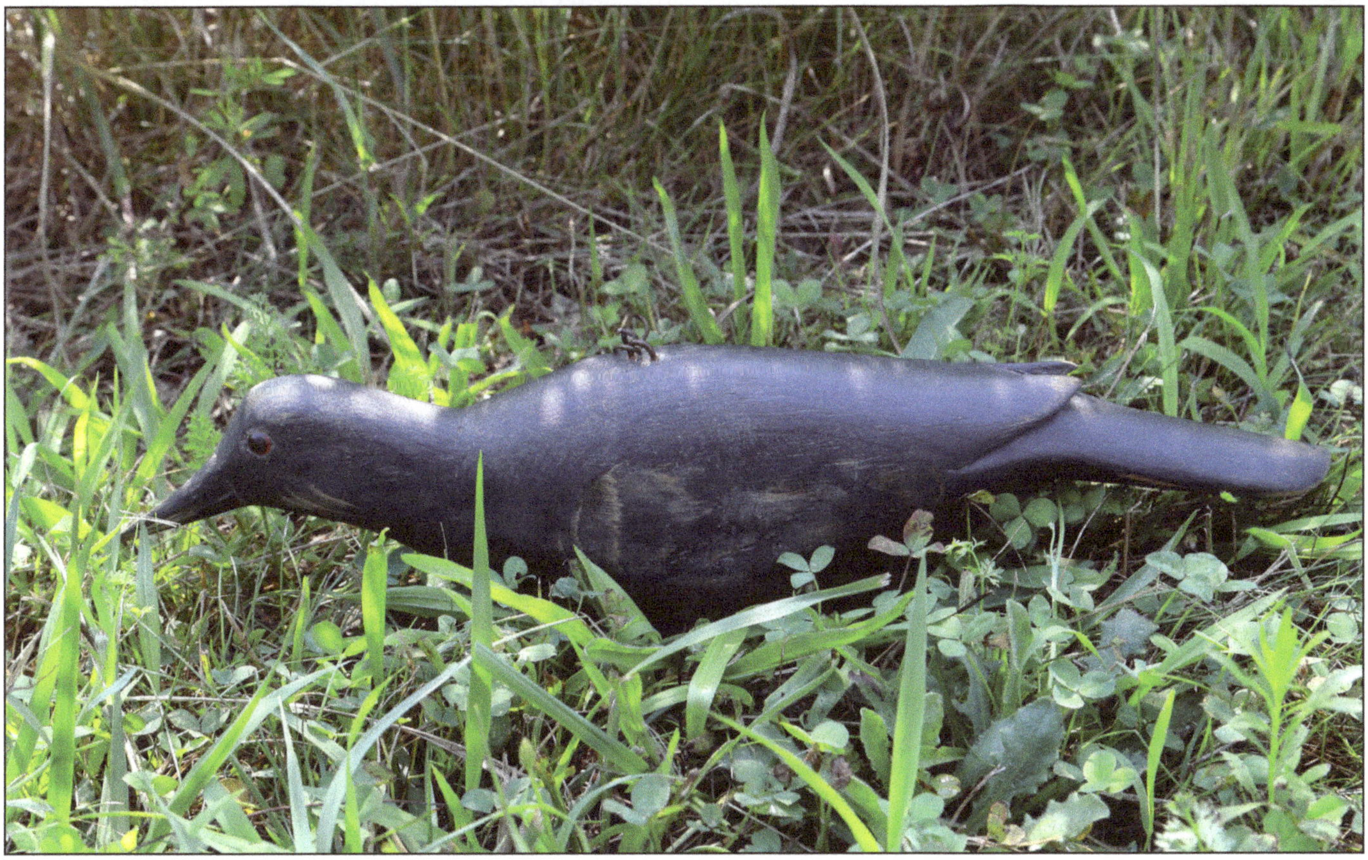

Blue Bill (this page)
This Blue Bill decoy, carved by Rowley Horner, is similar in style to decoys by the famous Harry Shourds, one of the area's most prolific carvers, except that Horner's ducks are a bit sleeker. One can tell a Horner decoy by checking the bill. At the bottom of the bill, Horner carves on an angle, like signing his name. This decoy, from Tuckerton, New Jersey, is very valuable.

Yellow Leg (next page)
This decoy is by Charles "Shang" Wheeler, a famous maker who hailed from Connecticut. It's a testament to Wheeler's personal style, particularly in the raised wing, as well as the split in the tail. When a carver added this defining touch, it made the decoy even more valuable. Some of the other birds we see have smooth wings, but Wheeler carved this in.

Pintail (pair)
This pair of ducks, hen and drake (from left to right), were carved by the Ward brothers, Steve and Lem, of Crisfield, Maryland. They are very valuable and, in my opinion, are the best of Fred's collection. I remember helping Fred buy them for only $150 apiece.

Fred and I had signals that we used when evaluating decoys, because dealers would come to Fred to sell him decoys and one time he bought a fake one, and I couldn't say anything in front of the dealer. So I called Fred the next day and said, "You and me, we got to get together. I let you buy a fake." I explained how I knew and my reasoning and we agreed on a set of signals that meant "buy more," "cut off," or "we don't need this one." To say "no" to a dealer, you would have to have a reason, and I wasn't going to give away my information about what I knew of decoys to some smart dealer.

The Ward brothers carved all species. Their decoys are just absolutely, drop-dead gorgeous. I got to meet the brothers one time. I went down to Lem Ward's one day and I got to talking to him. I told him he had a beautiful style about his decoys, the back of the neck has this Lem Ward curve. And he said to me, "How do you draw your decoys? Do you draw them left to right or right to left?" Then he took his pencil and showed me how he threw his curve, backwards, from the top of the neck to the nape, and it gave the beautiful Lem Ward curve. It is just beautiful. The eyes of this decoy are inset a little and have glass eyes, as taxidermist supplies were available to carvers. Eyes help date decoys, and show that these were made around 1930.

The old time decoy makers had sharp tools and ways to keep them sharp. When you talk about hand tools, the saying goes, a sharp tool will do what you want it to do; a dull tool will hurt you. So all their tools were sharp. They had sharpening methods for everything; they had oil stones and whetstones to keep their edges sharp. Most of the early tools were made out of carbon steel, which means it could be sharpened, even with a file. You could file it down and then hone it to a sharpness that is unbelievable. All the tools today, after World War II, are made with this Rockwell steel. It is stainless steel, case-hardened, and they sharpen differently. It's just something that old tools are easy to sharpen because they are made of carbon steel.

Canada Goose (this page)
This is a beautiful Canada Goose, made by Taylor Johnson around 1880 in Barnegat, New Jersey. It is about twenty-six inches long, making it a larger decoy, and made out of hollow cedar in a paddle-like shape, which is a Truex-type shape. The head is in the style of early Barnegat decoys.

At one point Fred Noyes had 3,500 decoys. Today in the Noyes Museum of Art of Stockton University 350 decoys remain. Fred would meet dealers at his home. He kept his decoys in his house on string. They were tied to the rafters and the ceiling joists. Many of them were still in barrels and barrels and barrels. It was just so much fun. Fred would call me up and say "Gary there's a guy here and he wants to sell me some decoys." And I would say, "I'll be over there in two minutes." Growing in knowledge about decoys with Fred was such fun. We grew together.

Red Knot (Dowitcher) (next page)
This Red Knot (Dowitcher) decoy is carved by Boyce. The decoy is distinguishable as a Red Knot by its shorter bill and red breast. Shot holes can be seen in this decoy. Hunters used to ground-swipe these birds. When the birds flew into the flock on the shore, they just got a big bunch of them together and shot. This left some shore birds dead, a few injured, and a couple flying away. Shore birds that hunters would shoot like this were not only good for meat, the breast and thigh meat on Red Knots, but also for sale to the millinery trade in the 1800s: the feathers were used for fancy hats. I recall a picture of a woman who wore a whole swan on her head, "wings and all."

Trumpeter Swan (this page)
When I first saw this swan I fell in love with it because it was so folky. I didn't care how much it was, I thought we should have it. I remember standing with Fred and the dealer and giving the "go more sign" to Fred. Originally from Maryland, the trumpeter swan is perhaps the biggest decoy in the collection. It is distinguished from other varieties of swan, such as the whistling swan, by its bill. A trumpeter's bill will be all black, while a whistling swan will have a yellow/orange knob on the top of its bill. This decoy is easy to fall in love with: it is extreme folk art at its best.

These three images (and the three on the following pages) are from original photographs made to record each decoy's appearance at the time of purchase.

Eider (next page top)
Here is an interesting decoy from the state of Maine. This is an Eider, similar to a Scoter. In Maine, they inlet the head of decoys into the body—see the head is inset—so it's very easy to distinguish a Maine decoy. This decoy has a cracked neck which has been repaired with a wooden dowel. It is all hand painted, probably with regular house paint. Old-time carvers would use whatever was at hand: "there's an old can of black; there's an old can of white." It was carved by Gus Wilson, around or just before 1920.

Black Duck (next page bottom)
This decoy is a Jersey Black Duck, carved by Harry Vanuckson Shourds out of Tuckerton, New Jersey, in 1900. Thicker than most, the shape of Shourds' decoys results, in part, from the materials he used. Cedar trees grow wider in shape towards the roots—they have bell bottoms—and sawyers, like my grandpop, would trim this excess leaving slabs of cedar about four-foot long. Grandpop would throw the slabs under the carriage for the decoy makers. This is where I met them, because they came to our sawmill to get the slabs: decoy carvers John Updike and Jake Barrett from Somers Point. Starting with such cedar slabs contributed to the signature shape that is characteristic of the Shourds Black Duck.

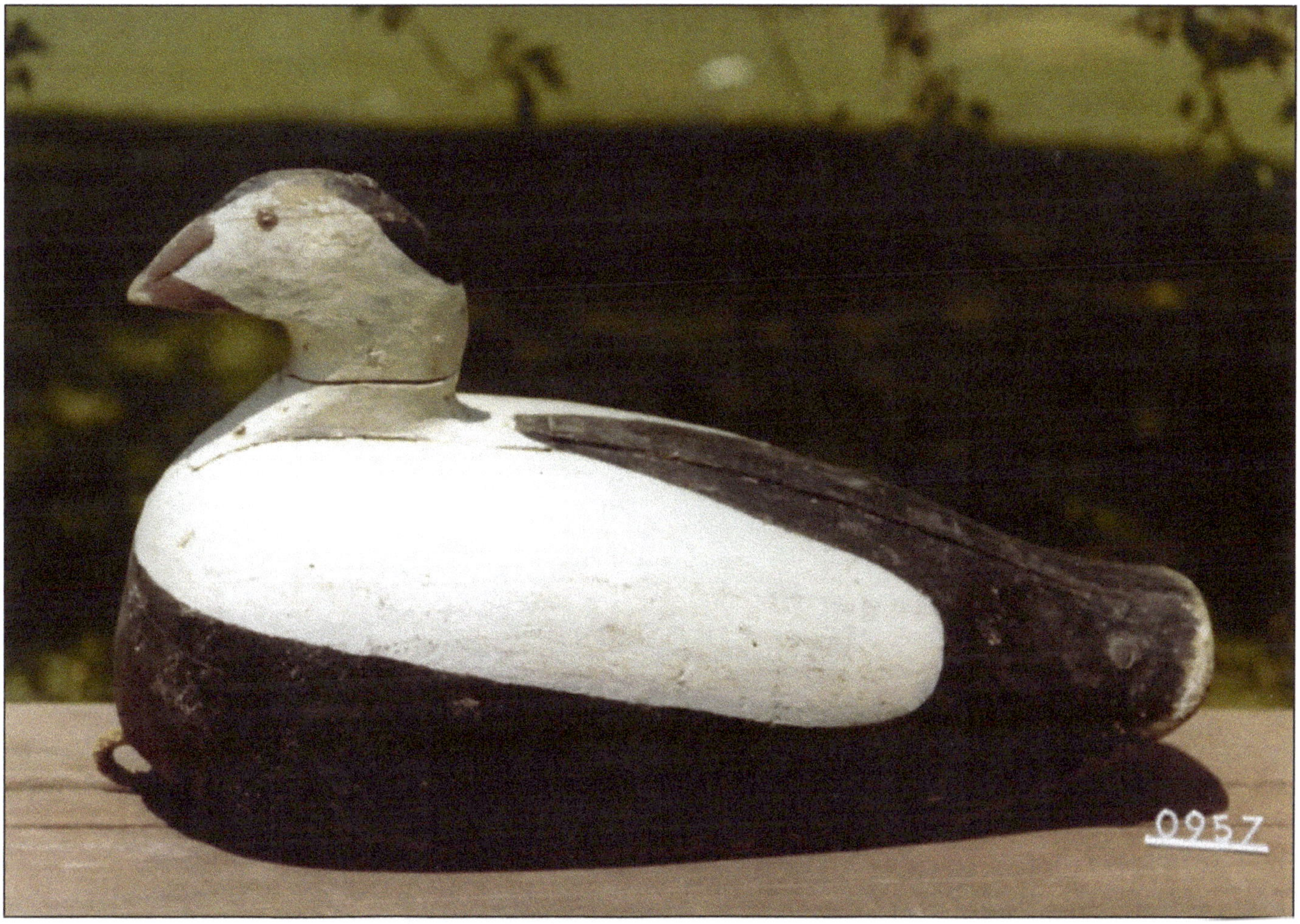

447

Merganser (this page)
This decoy is made by C. R. Huey in Friendship Island, Maine. It is a red breasted merganser. See the carved eye. What's neat about this duck is on the bottom. Huey stamped his name and a little blind duck. It's easy to spot the Huey merganser because it has a unique style, but there's no missing it when you turn it over and see the signature. This decoy dates to 1900 and is quite rare. Huey only made ducks for his personal use.

Base of Merganser (next page top)
Visible on the bottom of this decoy: the name stamp of C. R. Huey and two of duck images. Also visible is Fred Noyes' identification stamp, 199.

Golden Eye (next page bottom)
The trained eye can see and determine that the bill on this decoy was broken off and replaced at a later date. The original date of carving is 1880 by Captain Dan Showell of Absecon, New Jersey. This is one of the earlier decoys to be found in the collection.

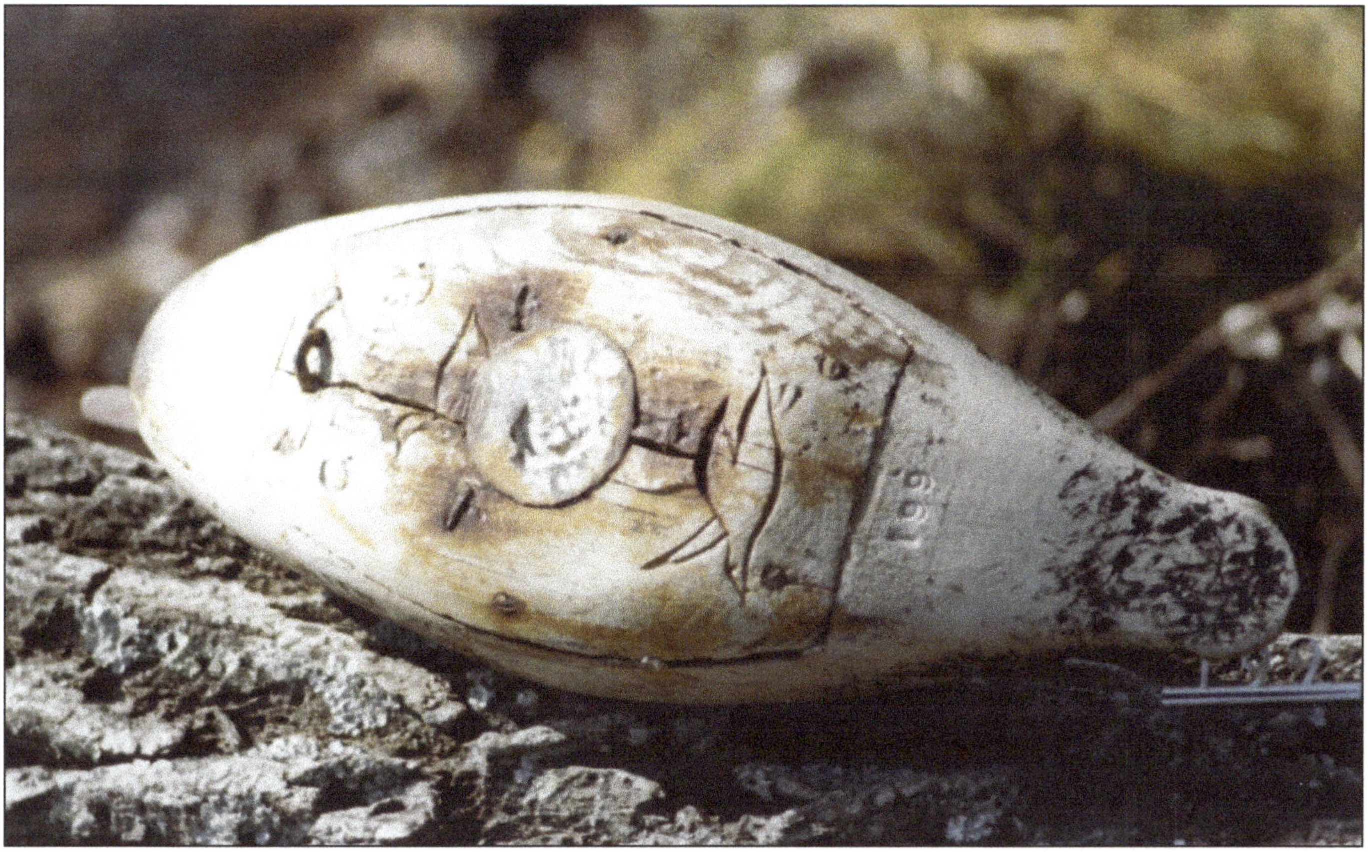

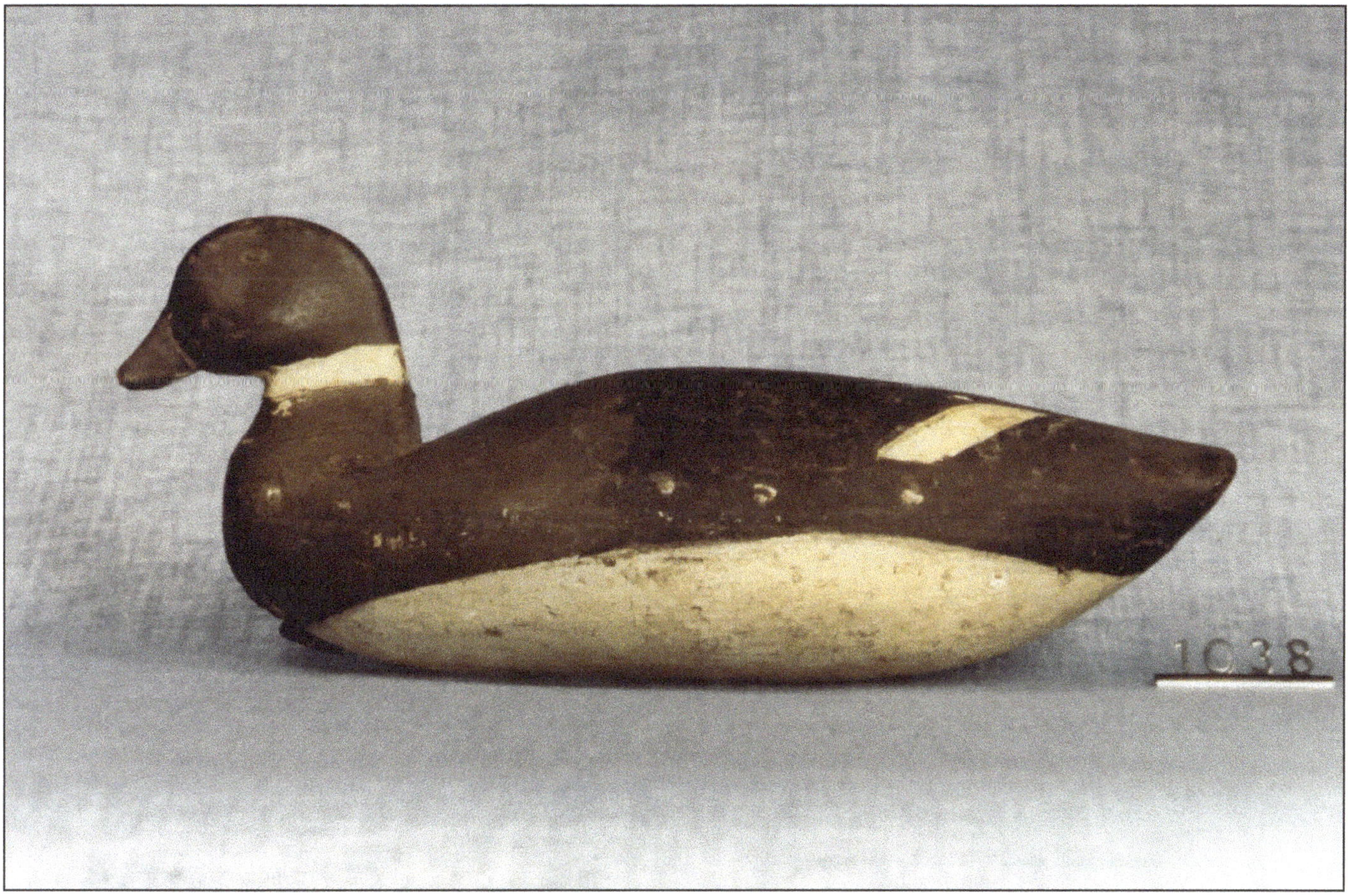

Fred Noyes Jr. and Mackey
This is a great picture of Fred. He was in a good mood that day. He has his Greek fisherman's hat on, which he loved to wear. He's fondling his little dog Mackey, but Mackey was a mean thing; he bit so many people; he bit my wife. Fred named him after William J. Mackey Jr., the biggest decoy collector of his time, whom Fred bought many of his birds from.

Fred Noyes and Nikki Giberson cataloging decoys. Nikki is holding a decoy as Fred stamps identification numbers on the bottom.

Gary Giberson's First Decoys

I started carving in 1948. My father went over to Marine Mart in Atlantic City to buy some decoys, because our decoys were stolen. Marine Mart was a beautiful store up in the old inlet; I think it was on Gramercy Avenue and Massachusetts. And when you opened the door to the store, all you could smell was steam tar. They steam tarred the rope; they steam tarred the string; they steam tarred the nets. Don't ask me how they did it. I would love to know how they steam tarred. They steam tarred everything. So when you opened the door that smell hits you. And they had everything in there. All the furnishings you needed for a boat, from all the propellers, the rudders, the shafts—they didn't sell engines there—but you could buy anything else you wanted for a boat. All the gear, the ropes, the chocks—anything you needed to put on a boat or build a boat—including decoys for hunting.

So my father came back with this rig of J. W. Bowen decoys. They had little teeny heads and great big bodies, and I said to my father, "They'll scare more ducks than they attract. They are so ugly." And he said to me, "Well if you think they're so ugly, why don't you get together with your grandpop across the street and make some decoys?" So I did.

I went across the street and grandpop helped me. He band-sawed the heads out for me and showed me how to carve and how to chop the bodies with a hatchet and then shape them with a rasp and how to build a unique bench called a schnitzelbunk—it's German so it's spelled exactly how it sounds, otherwise I'm the worst speller—but I used the schnitzelbunk. So I made this dozen decoys for my father and there was this State Police Captain who gunned with our neighbor down the end of the road and he come down and saw my decoys on the back of my father's boat and asked if he could buy them.

Well, I run home really quick, it was just down the road here a ways, I run home really quick and said, "Daddy, can I sell those decoys, I can make you some more." And he said, "Sure go ahead, does someone want to buy them?" So I went back and I knew that Updike and Hendrickson were selling decoys up the Mullica River and they were getting thirty dollars a dozen for 'em, so I decided I would want a little more than them, so I got thirty-two dollars a dozen.

"And how old were you?"

1948—thirteen years old.

Learning about Decoys. Gary Giberson, Mayor of Port Republic, New Jersey, and long-time decoy carver, describes the Noyes collection to Claire Riley, Tom Kinsella, and Shannon Stolz.

THE GAME SEASON.

There is excellent shooting on the Jersey bays just now, and sportsmen should go there early before the birds become wild. Black ducks, mud hens, mallards and teal are plenty, and redheads, bluebills and whistlers will arrive within a week. Snipe still frequent the flats at low water, but are hard to reach. Barnegat is the most favorite resort for wild fowl, particularly brant. Sportsmen must remember, however, that the law forbids the placing of decoys more than three rods from the edge of the marsh, the pursuing of game after dark with a light, or Sunday shooting. The fowl now to be had are young and quite tame, and can be paddled on quite easily. Good rail shooting is still to be had, although many of these birds have gone South. The second brood of quail are found, but the birds are in very poor condition and very small. The open season for this game, however, is not until November 1st.

But few deer are killed now, although the game is plenty and in good condition. A buck, the largest ever seen in South Jersey, was captured a few days ago by Alfred Mathis, of Franklinville. It weighed 258 pounds, and was killed near Beaver Dam. Fishing is about over, and is chiefly confined to creeks and rivers. Striped bass weighing from half a pound to two pounds, and a few blues are the chief results.

From *The Bridgeton Pioneer*, October 29, 1885, 4.

Swan Bay Jim
Gasoline Seventeen Cents a Gallon; Moonshine a Dollar a Quart
By Gary B. Giberson

Enjoy two stories by Gary B. Giberson, long-time Mayor of Port Republic, master decoy carver, entrepreneur, and author. Printed in flip-book format, here are two short stories with illustrations by distinguished artist Kathy Anne English and photographs by Giberson. Follow an impossible hunt through the cedar swamps of the Mullica River and join an adventurous chase to capture rum-runners during Prohibition.

40 pages, paperback.
ISBN: 978-0-9976699-4-7.
Available at Second Time Books, Mount Laurel, and Amazon.

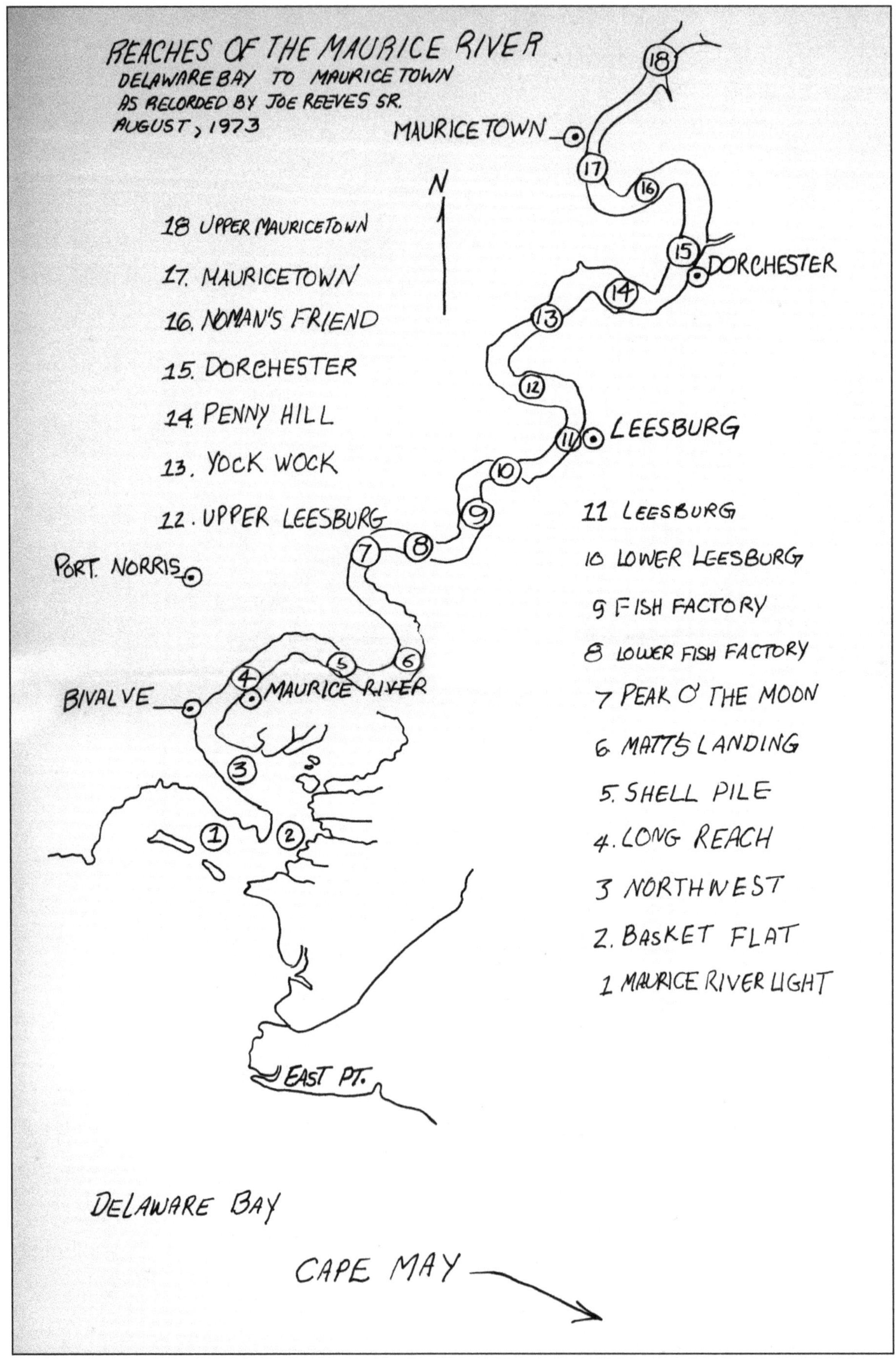
REACHES OF THE MAURICE RIVER
DELAWARE BAY TO MAURICE TOWN
AS RECORDED BY JOE REEVES SR.
AUGUST, 1973
MAURICETOWN
N
18 UPPER MAURICETOWN
17. MAURICETOWN
16. NOMAN'S FRIEND
15. DORCHESTER
14. PENNY HILL
13. YOCK WOCK
12. UPPER LEESBURG
DORCHESTER
LEESBURG
PORT. NORRIS
11 LEESBURG
10 LOWER LEESBURG
9 FISH FACTORY
8 LOWER FISH FACTORY
7 PEAK O' THE MOON
6 MATTS LANDING
5. SHELL PILE
4. LONG REACH
3 NORTHWEST
2. BASKET FLAT
1 MAURICE RIVER LIGHT
BIVALVE
MAURICE RIVER
EAST PT.
DELAWARE BAY
CAPE MAY

Maurice River Memories:
"Driftwood" and "Start of the Season"

Joseph S. Reeves Jr.

Driftwood[1]

I wanted to pick beans in my vegetable garden early in the morning but the dew was still on the plants and mosquitoes would have eaten me alive. I needed a haircut anyway and walked the short distance to Pete Tribett's barber shop. His shop was in the front part of Duly Campbell's house only a half block up the street. I sat on the wood settee inside while Pete finished shaving Walter Hinson. The barber used Mr. Hinson's personal shaving mug and brush to make and apply lather. Monogrammed mugs belonging to local area men were arrayed on narrow wood shelves. The shelves were placed on both sides of a large mirror. While Pete cut my hair, I looked out the bay window and saw Ida G. and Carolyn Bacon working on their lawn in the shade of tall elms directly across the street. Al Hilliard came in about the time my haircut was done. I paid the usual twenty-five cents and walked back to the house.

My dad was applying a coat of paint to his railbirding skiff, which was perched on wooden saw horses in our side yard. He'd be putting the boat in the river soon because the season, which begins on September 1st, was only three weeks away. When he finished the painting we headed for the wharf, with the intention of picking up driftwood downriver. The wood provided much of our fuel for the iron range in the kitchen. This was our only source of heat in winter. We took the big bateau because it would hold more. The tide had been coming up for about two hours, so we'd have to buck the current.

Dad rowed downriver along the west bank and we started picking up floating driftwood right after passing the first sluice gate into the lower meadow. We rowed along the bank following the shore line as it curved northeastward into Noman's Friend Reach. The driftwood was caught in the rushes growing near the riverbank. Much of it was scrap lumber from the shipyards in Mauricetown, Dorchester and Leesburg. It was waterlogged and very heavy and would not be good for firewood until dry. By the time we reached the downriver end of Noman's Friend the boat was loaded, so we pulled into the riverbank and piled the driftwood on the dike. After a week or two, when it had dried and become much lighter, we'd come back to retrieve it.

I got on the oar's and we continued, rounding the bend into Dorchester Reach. We saw a pile driver working near the Dorchester shipyard and thought Uncle John McClain, Mom's younger brother, might be operating it, so we crossed over to the east side of the river. A ninety-foot navy submarine chaser was being constructed on the yard's ways. Her hull was nearing completion but no paint had yet been applied to the new oak lumber. We stayed a few yards offshore but could see Johnny operating some long levers. The pile driver's big steel hammer slammed down again and again, driving a tall wood piling into the river bottom. The operator's cab and all the machinery was mounted on a huge wood float which rocked every time the hammer came down,

1 *This is the second installment of Joseph S. Reeves Jr.'s stories, first published in his* Maurice River Memories *(1993). The work is a collection of his childhood experiences on the Maurice River with his family and shows a bygone era of railbird hunting, fishing, and turtle trapping. These stories are republished in* SoJourn *with the kind permission of the Mauricetown Historical Society, the copyright holder. The accompanying illustrations, including the map to the left, are from the original printing.*

sending little waves across the water. The piling was part of a new wharf being constructed near the yard. Johnny saw us waving at him, stopped the machine, came out of the operator's cab and waved back. Uncle John was a great guy. I thought he must be one lucky person, to operate big machinery all the time.

My sisters and I always looked forward to Uncle John's regular visits when we were little kids. He was very reliable. On those days when we knew he would visit we'd keep looking across the river. As we played in our backyard, we could see all the cars moving along the Station Road toward the bridge. There wasn't much traffic so we could nearly always pick out his car. It was very easy when he got his 1936 yellow Chevrolet because nearly all cars were black or gray in those days. When we saw his car we would dance around and yell a lot for the few minutes it took him to arrive.

We waved at Uncle John again, then rowed back across the river to search for more driftwood. A lot of oak wedges floated along the shore line. These came from ship launchings. They were just the right size for our stove. Every now and then we found a piece of really good lumber like a 2 x 12 x 16-foot plank. We wouldn't cut these into firewood because they came in handy for other purposes. We found what looked like a hatch cover from a schooner's hold. It was heavy, so we put it up on the bank at the spot where we'd found it. We kept rowing downriver to the lower end of Penny Hill Reach, collecting another boatload. The tide was still coming in and would keep coming in for another hour or so.

Dad wanted favoring tide for the row back, so he decided to turn around where Penny Hill bends into Yock Wock Reach. Just then we saw a large object close to the riverbank and partially hidden by sawgrass. Investigating further, we discovered a rowboat floating submerged to its gunwales. It was very muddy and at first glance appeared worthless, but on closer inspection it looked salvageable. It must have drifted into this location and been trapped here for some time. We needed to get the water out of the sunken boat to take a better look at it. Dad used an oar as a lever against the bottom, about two feet deep here, and pried the boat toward the bank. He managed to get its sides just enough above the surface, about an inch, to start bailing. All we had in our boat was a large juice can, so we started taking turns. At first we bailed by leaning over from our boat. After ten minutes or so, we had about three inches of freeboard. We then knew water was not leaking in faster than we could bail. The boat kept looking better as more of it floated above the surface, although it had collected much mud and silt. After a while, enough of it was above water, so dad climbed into it, which enabled him to bail faster. Finally, I stepped in and took a turn bailing the last of the water. The boat appeared not to be leaking at all. Furthermore, it looked very sound, not an old boat at all. Even its paint under all the mud was in fair condition. Only about two feet of painter remained attached, the end torn and frayed. Someone had probably tied up at high tide, not leaving enough slack, and the weight of the boat had snapped the painter when the tide fell.

Dad took the painter from our boat and rigged a tow line. We had used a lot of time bailing but the tide was still coming in, so we would get some help on the first part of the tow. Heading back upriver with the sixteen-foot boat in tow, we noticed it tended to slew around somewhat and Dad said he thought its skag might be damaged. It floated well and took no water; in fact it was even drying out inside. We passed Dorchester Shipyard and turned up Noman's Friend at peak flood tide. Dad pulled into the bank, where we cached the driftwood, and off-loaded the rest of our collection there. The tow was easier with the heavy driftwood unloaded but the tide began ebbing and we had to row into the current.

I rowed awhile but my left ankle was itching so Dad rowed while I removed my boot and scratched the itchy spot. We had picked wild huckleberries the day before and chiggers must have bitten me. Our pants had been tied around the ankles but some of the bugs had gotten through anyway. We had walked the mile from town across the Station Road to Mauricetown railroad station. Then we picked berries while walking south along the tracks almost to Dorchester station. About a quarter mile down the tracks we flushed a ruffed grouse from under a big clump of ferns. The bird startled us when it exploded out of the brush nearly underfoot. We didn't routinely see grouse around the meadows, because they liked dry areas with lots of cover.

Dad stayed near the north shore line heading up Noman's Friend. With the tide ebbing, the current was stronger on the opposite side. Part way up Mauricetown Reach we angled over to the town side. By the time we reached our wharf the salvaged boat was doing well, with no leaks. After tying up, we felt under the stern, discovering that the skag was broken off. Of all the parts of a boat that might need repair, this was probably the easiest to mend. There were no markings. That was no surprise, because hardly anyone painted a name or number on a rowboat. We always associated a boat with its owner by its appearance—like matching a face with a person.

We grabbed a bite to eat, then Dad headed back to the wharf to scrub the mud from the boat's interior. He'd have to wait for the next high tide to pull it out on the wharf to look over its bottom and repair the skag. It was still very hot but I picked the beans. They were very plentiful, so Mom could put some up for the winter. I enjoyed working in the garden. The rich, black soil was easy to work, wet or dry, and the little backyard plot produced plenty of vegetables. I pulled every weed in sight and checked for insect pests. I used no chemicals, because they were too expensive. I could keep the bugs under control by checking the underside of plant leaves, smashing egg clusters and picking off bugs and larvae with my fingers. I harvested three yellow crook-necked squash and several big red tomatoes for Mom, then got ready to deliver newspapers.

I had taken over the town's only paper route from Melville Burford a few months back. My customers were just about everybody in town: I delivered about 115 papers. About two thirds of the people took the *Philadelphia Bulletin*; only six took the *Camden Courier*. Some folks took the *Bridgeton Evening News* or the *Millville Republican*. I delivered two papers at some houses. *The Bulletin* and *Courier* were 3 cents and the local papers were 2 cents. I made 1 cent on each paper, six days a week. I didn't handle *The Philadelphia Inquirer* delivered on Sundays.

I heard the truck stop briefly and dump the bundles of newspapers in our front yard. My bike was leaning up against the back of the house so I moved it out front. I cut the string from around the roll of newspapers and checked the headlines for August 10, 1940: "GERMAN BOMBERS STRIKE ENGLAND AGAIN—SPITFIRES DOWN SIX PLANES." I loaded the light local papers in the wire basket over the front wheel. I carried the *Bulletin* and *Courier* in a cloth pouch slung over my shoulder. Tom Robbins came across the street to get his paper. He couldn't wait until I delivered it because, although he lived close, he was the last stop on my route. I always started toward the Buckshutem road first. I never used rubber bands, because nearly everyone had a picket fence. It was easy to ride up on the bike and wedge the paper in the fence near the front gate. If they didn't have a fence, I would lay it on the front porch or, on a windy day, put it behind the screen door. Many times people would be out waiting for me to deliver, especially if they were really interested in the war news.

There were several men hanging around Joe Sharp's garage, talking about the war. Herb Robbins, Russell Berry, Frosty Bradway and Steve Shropshire were going over the toll of ships sunk by German submarines. Joe Sharp was pumping gas into my Uncle Morty's 1935 Ford sedan. The price on a sign above the pump was 19.9 cents per gallon. I could have drunk a big bottle of Pepsi Cola but I didn't want to spend the nickel and couldn't drink it while I had a full load of papers, so I went on. Mrs. Compton was in her yard, so I handed her the paper. She always tried to engage me in conversation and acted as though she were my mother—kind of gushing all over me a lot.

Arthur Hinson' s was the last house on the Buckshutem road, almost a mile from home. I always worried about delivering there, because he had a Great Dane. The dog hadn't figured out yet that he could jump the white picket fence if he wanted to. He would start barking when I was well down the road, leaping about behind the fence and keeping me in a sweat. I would ride up and slip the rolled-up paper in the fence just a few inches from his nose. I wondered when he would decide to jump. He stood higher than the fence so it would have been easy. He never did. On Saturdays when I came to collect I'd just sit on my bike out front until Mrs. Lizzy Hinson, attracted by the racket, came out and paid me. If the dog wasn't out, it was necessary to enter the yard and knock on the front door. At these times I would try to see if the dog was around back waiting to come around the corner of the house after me. I was either lucky or careful; we never had an encounter.

On the way past Boyden Robbins' store I noticed several people gathered at the post office. This was the social center of town. I handed some of them their paper. I continued delivering up the main street until I reached my last customer, Frank Feaster, who lived in the next-to-last house on the Haleyville road. On the route back I saw Mr. Burford, who was back in town after a long absence. He would disappear for months at a time, even years. I finished by delivering to the back street, ending up on our block.

I saw Grandad Reeves feeding his hunting dogs and handed him the paper. The two Irish Setters were wolfing down their meal from a big bowl of dried dog food. I couldn't help thinking about the dog food incident from a few days before. Grandad Reeves had decided that it was a lot of trouble to mix the dog food with water every feeding time. Why not mix the entire 25 pound bag with water in a big washtub in advance?

He'd ladle out each meal from the tub as needed. When the water was combined with a full bag the mixture filled a large steel galvanized tub nearly to the brim. Unexpected results followed. In the summer's heat the mixture began to produce bubbles—and an obnoxious odor. The dogs would have no part of it and the entire mess was thrown into the river. My grandfather reverted to preparing each meal separately.

Later that evening a lot of townfolk gathered in the firehouse for a lesson in first aid. The town firehouse, on the corner of Noble Street and Stable Lane, had been converted from what had been a store in years past. Before the lesson got underway, Frosty Bradway moved the red fire truck out of the way. I thought Frosty made a lot of fuss doing it because everybody was standing around watching him operate the big old 1928 engine and he enjoyed the attention. Austin Hiles, Billy Estell and some of the other volunteer firemen were on hand, trying to look important. They got in the act by issuing a few orders while the fire engine was being moved out. The first aid lesson was good, though. There was a lot of interest because the European War had been going on for a year. The war wasn't that far away either; there were reports every day about ships being torpedoed. Some sinkings were very close to the Jersey coast. Somebody got up after the lesson and asked everybody who owned a car to paint the top half of their headlights black, since we might have blackouts.

It took me a while to get to sleep that night; the humidity was high and the house held the heat. There wasn't a breath of air stirring. As I was about to doze off, a cat fight broke out in our back yard and woke me back up again. Then I heard distant thunder, which became louder and more frequent. The wind picked up and lightning flashes accompanied the thunder. I must have gone to sleep because I don't remember when the rain started.

Maurice River Memories

Start of the Season

My dad knelt on one knee at the boat's stern and motioned for me to ease our bateau further out into the river. He was selecting the spot to begin laying off a gill net. Our boat was at the downriver end of Noman's Friend Reach just above the bend from Dorchester. One man alone would have started from the north side of the river, allowing the wind to drift the boat across while he dispersed the net. With a helper rowing, a shad fisherman could pass the net off the stern as the boat was rowed across the river into the wind. The incoming tide was about two hours old and the weather wasn't good. An intermittent light drizzle fell and a cold wind blew in gusts from the northeast.

It was a Saturday morning in the third week of April, 1941; a bit early for shad. My dad had caught the first of the spring run the previous week. The big runs hadn't come up river yet. It wasn't a good day to be out but it had been a long cold winter and our cupboard was bare.

Noman's Friend was well named. No sooner did we get the two hundred foot long drift net placed across the river than the swirling currents displaced it. The fast moving current on the north side of the reach caused that end to outpace the opposite end caught in backwater on the south side. Halfway up the reach the net was aligned lengthwise up and down the river in mid-stream. This was not the best way to present a barrier to the fish run, but if we overtended the net by constantly towing it, our chances of a catch would be decreased. The net began to bunch up where the tricky currents in the reach formed eddies. Several cork floats bobbed and some went under almost like they do when fish strike. The action was typical of this reach when the tide was running strong. At the tender age of fifteen (almost), I was still fooled by the effect of the currents on the net. My dad waited patiently.

Nearly two thirds of the way up the reach there was a strike! The fifth cork in from the upriver end. Now again! This time two corks were bobbing under! Still on the oars, I rowed over to the spot and Dad very gently eased up that section of net. First one, then another large roe shad, about five or six pounds each, came into view. Both were entangled in the fine thread gill net. One of the fish was badly entangled.

The tide was moving us rapidly upriver. We were fast approaching the bend into Mauricetown Reach where the river nearly doubles back on itself. Very soon we would have to swing the long net around the point of the bend by towing it. If not, the strong tide and northeast wind would ground the net on river bottom fasts (snags) near the far bank, ripping it to shreds. A look at the far line of trees well beyond the riverbank showed that we were drifting upstream at an alarming rate. I could see my dad occasionally glance up at the approaching river bend as he worked on what appeared to me to be hopelessly entangled fish. I held the boat's position over the net while he diligently worked over the side in the raw cold wind. Had it been me, I would have torn the fine threads from around the fish, leaving at least a six-foot hole and a two-day repair job. Then I saw that the waterman's skill with the net matched his judgment. He freed one fish quickly and now, with time running out, the tangle suddenly came away from the second. The fish, gripped tightly by the head in one hand, was thrown into the boat along with the first and the untangled net lowered back into the water.

Then my dad took the oars. As I shifted to the stern seat he quickly rowed to the upriver end of the net. I fished the buoy from the water and braced it under the stern seat while he turned the boat toward the point of the river bend. With one foot firmly braced against the stern seat support he began the hard tow to swing the gill net around this sharp bend. On this day it would be more difficult than usual. The strong northeast wind blowing directly off the point joined forces with the fast-moving tide to try to send the gill net to its demise in the fasts along the river bottom near the opposite shore. It would be a test of strength and endurance that the waterman had undergone hundreds of times before. He hadn't always been successful though, having struck the fasts several times over the years. He was rowing hard now, oars biting deep into the water with every stroke. The net strung out taut behind us with the far end still curving downriver like a huge whip.

Joe Reeves was in good physical condition at the age of forty-three. Years of rowing had given him fine upper-body strength and endurance. He wasn't breathing hard, just working hard. Halfway around the bend we were holding our own—rowing stroke after stroke, the waterman at the oars with the long gill net in tow. We were in a standoff with the wind and the tide—the oars visibly bending with each hard pull. Would one of them break?

Gradually, we swung the bend and were now gaining a bit. The cork floats became evenly spaced and lined up all the way to the far end of the net. My dad slowed his pace, then backed on the oars and relaxed. The gill net went slack and was in perfect position across the river for the drift up Mauricetown Reach. With any luck the big shad runs would be getting underway soon.

Maurice River Shad Fishing

My dad, Joe Reeves, was a waterman who knew the Maurice River well. Using his knowledge of the river, he earned our family's livelihood with a rowboat and a pair of oars. I started fishing with my dad when I was about thirteen, in 1939. He would let me go only on days when there was no school. Shad season was the best time on the river. We fished for shad during the spring when the fish came upriver to spawn. The first fish was normally caught around mid April. The number of shad in the river increased in late April, then hit a peak around the first or second week of May. After that the catch declined; it ended in the first week of June. Roe shad were definitely preferred over bucks. The roe made a delicious meal by itself. The fish was very good to eat although boney. An average roe shad weighs about four to five pounds but can range in size up to six or even seven pounds. The bucks are smaller, averaging somewhat more than three pounds.

My dad and his brothers caught shad with gill nets. We drifted the nets in the tidal reaches of the Maurice River. Sometimes rockfish were taken while drifting for shad. Large rock could damage the fine threaded nets. My dad told me many stories about catching sturgeon in his drift nets in the early part of the 20th century. Sturgeon became scarce but I can remember Dad catching one in 1942. The fish weighed more than 200 pounds. Dad knew the proper method required to pack the roe with salt to produce caviar; he'd had prior experience. The damage to the drift net from catching a sturgeon was usually extensive and required at least a day to repair.

Gill nets used for shad were made from very fine linen thread. Their mesh size ranged from 5 & 1/8th inches in increments of 1/8th to 5 & 7/8ths. This measurement was taken diagonally, corner-to-corner, with the mesh stretched. The larger mesh size allowed small fish to slip through without being gilled. My dad normally selected 5 & 3/4 size. His catches were made up of good sized roe, with only a few bucks. The fine thread net was hung between lengths of 1/4 inch line. When finished it was about 200 feet long and 15 feet from cork line to lead line. The net was suspended by cork floats, attached with coarse twine, about every six feet. The float

leaders were adjusted to allow the net to be suspended at varying depths beneath the surface. In the reaches around Mauricetown, where the river was deep, the leaders were let full out, adding about three feet to the 15-foot depth. Upriver drifting called for less depth and there the float leaders were taken up a foot or two. The lead line was held down by small lead weights placed about four feet apart. The cork line was extended for about 15 feet on each end, ending with a (2 x 2 x 36 inch) wooden buoy.

After World War II nylon and other synthetic materials were used for nets. Linen was used during my years on the river. Normally, we got only one full season from a new net. It was possible to get part of another season if special care was taken to extend the net's life. The investment of about $30 was difficult to raise during the depression of the 1930s. Of course, the floats and leads were used repeatedly and the lines between which the net leash was hung could often be used for two seasons. My dad and his brothers were masters at hanging (making up) shad nets. The nets were prepared during the last part of winter or early spring, well before the start of the season in April.

We used an ordinary wooden rowboat or bateau when drifting for shad. These were flat bottom boats, fifteen to sixteen feet in length, tapered in the bow and squared off in the stern. The squared-off stern made a good platform for dispersing (laying off) the net and for taking it out of the water. About 1940 some of the fishermen got small outboard motors. They were useful in returning against the tide to begin another drift. My dad preferred to row and rarely used an outboard when shad fishing.

Much experience and knowledge of the river was essential to drift a gill net successfully. It was easy for the currents to drift the net into shallow water and allow it to become snagged or fast on a bottom hazard such as an old tree stump or sunken vessel. On the other hand, if the shad fisherman was too concerned and kept towing the net to avoid possible hazards, his ability to take fish was hampered. The tide ran strong most of the time, requiring the fisherman to negotiate the drift net around river bends. The tide's momentum always drifted the net directly toward the opposite shore. To counter this the fisherman towed the net toward the point of the river bend until it could drift up the next reach clear of shallow water. Sometimes the tow was very difficult, especially if the change in river direction between reaches was sharp, such as between Noman's Friend and Mauricetown reaches. Wind direction and speed could aggravate or lessen the tidal forces.

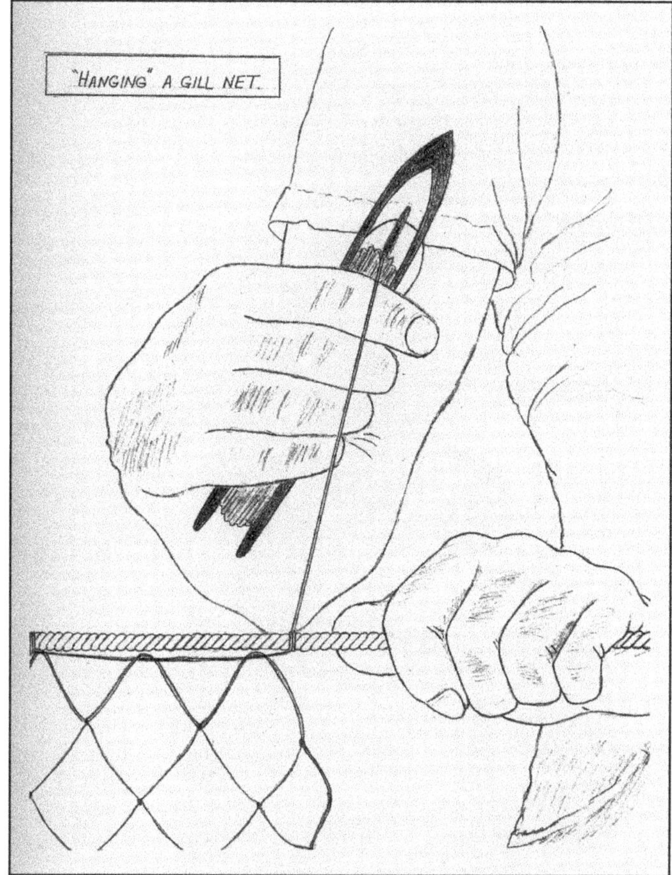

The Mauricetown bridge was a man-made hazard which ended all drifts from either direction. When I was first learning to drift with my dad I would become most concerned when the flood tide was drifting us upriver at a fast rate. We'd pass the shipyard, drifting toward the bridge, while my dad sat patiently waiting for that one last fish to strike before taking in the net. We always took in the last few fathoms of net as the tide swept us into the draw between the bridge piers.

Most of the work in fishing for shad took the form of rowing. When we were fishing the local reaches there was a lot of rowing between drifts to get back to a starting place for another drift. Towing the net around the river bends required hard rowing and stamina. I was about 15 years old before I had enough strength to handle this chore when the wind was wrong for the tow.

Fishing for shad also required a delicate touch. Taking a barely gilled fish out of the net without losing it was a skill learned the hard way. My dad could do this well. When a fish was well tangled anyone could take it. Sometimes, as the net was very gently drawn to the surface, a shad appeared to be caught by a single mesh. Patience was essential in such instances. I've seen

my dad take a fish when it wasn't actually caught but was just lying up against the net.

We were always prepared for larger fish. A steel gaff was carried in the boat and we used it occasionally. It was an absolute must for sturgeon and could come in handy for extra large rock of 30 pounds or more in getting them into the boat before their thrashing damaged the net extensively.

There was very little boat traffic on the river other than fishermen. In the 30's and 40's there were no pleasure boats. At times commercial traffic did present a problem. Oyster schooners moving up and down the river between shipyards or docks would sometimes interfere with the fishermen. Their tall masts could be seen several reaches away so we had plenty of warning. Now and then a cargo barge being moved by a tug would use the river when the fishermen were active. When this happened it was necessary to take the net up and go back for another drift. Commercial traffic always assumed they had the right of way. The fishermen made no argument because to leave the net in the water and risk having it severely damaged by a large vessel was foolhardy.

Upriver drifts were normally started in the morning on a day when flood tide came before noon. This allowed a drift up on the incoming tide and back on the ebb, thus cutting rowing time. The river was more shallow further up and the incoming tide provided deeper water. Actually, the better quality shad were caught in the lower reaches near Mauricetown. Fish in the upper reaches were nearer their spawning grounds. We fished many reaches on the Maurice River, from Leesburg down river to above Mud Haul upriver.

Much of the time we fished Noman's Friend or Mauricetown reaches. Noman's Friend Reach was usually tricky, with many crazy currents and eddies whenever there was much tide flowing. (This was most of the time.) We would often "lay off" in Noman's Friend on an upriver drift so we could have the net in the water and all set up at the beginning of Mauricetown Reach. Mauricetown Reach was smooth and stable and we caught more shad there.

We kept fish ready for sale in large wooden, sheet-metal lined, ice chests. Ours sat under the shade of a tree in the backyard. Many fish were sold to individuals. We also sold to dealers from fish markets in Bridgeton, Ocean City and elsewhere. We rarely had to ship fish out; the buyers came to us. During World War II when there were meat shortages shad sold very well. We never had a fish on hand for more than two days. Dad scaled and cleaned fish for anyone who asked, and most did. My mother cooked shad for us now and then, although to us they were a luxury we couldn't afford.

I look back on our shad seasons with fond memories. Although hard work was involved, there were many good times. Drifting the river on a warm May day with a lot of friends and relatives around was fun. My dad taught me well and let me first fish alone for a few drifts in 1943. I used a net which was still serviceable from the year before. We had dried it regularly after use and this extended its life for most of another year.

In addition to my dad the people who fished for shad around Mauricetown were his five brothers and a few other local men. Early in April, before the first sign of shad, they would stop by and talk with Dad about when to start drifting. Sometimes one of the men would try a drift with no luck, then give up for a day or two. We could see the river easily from our kitchen windows. I'd notice my dad looking at the river and pondering the sky during the first part of April. Then one day he would take his drift net and go out. Since I can first remember, it was my dad who took the first shad from the Maurice River at the start of every season.

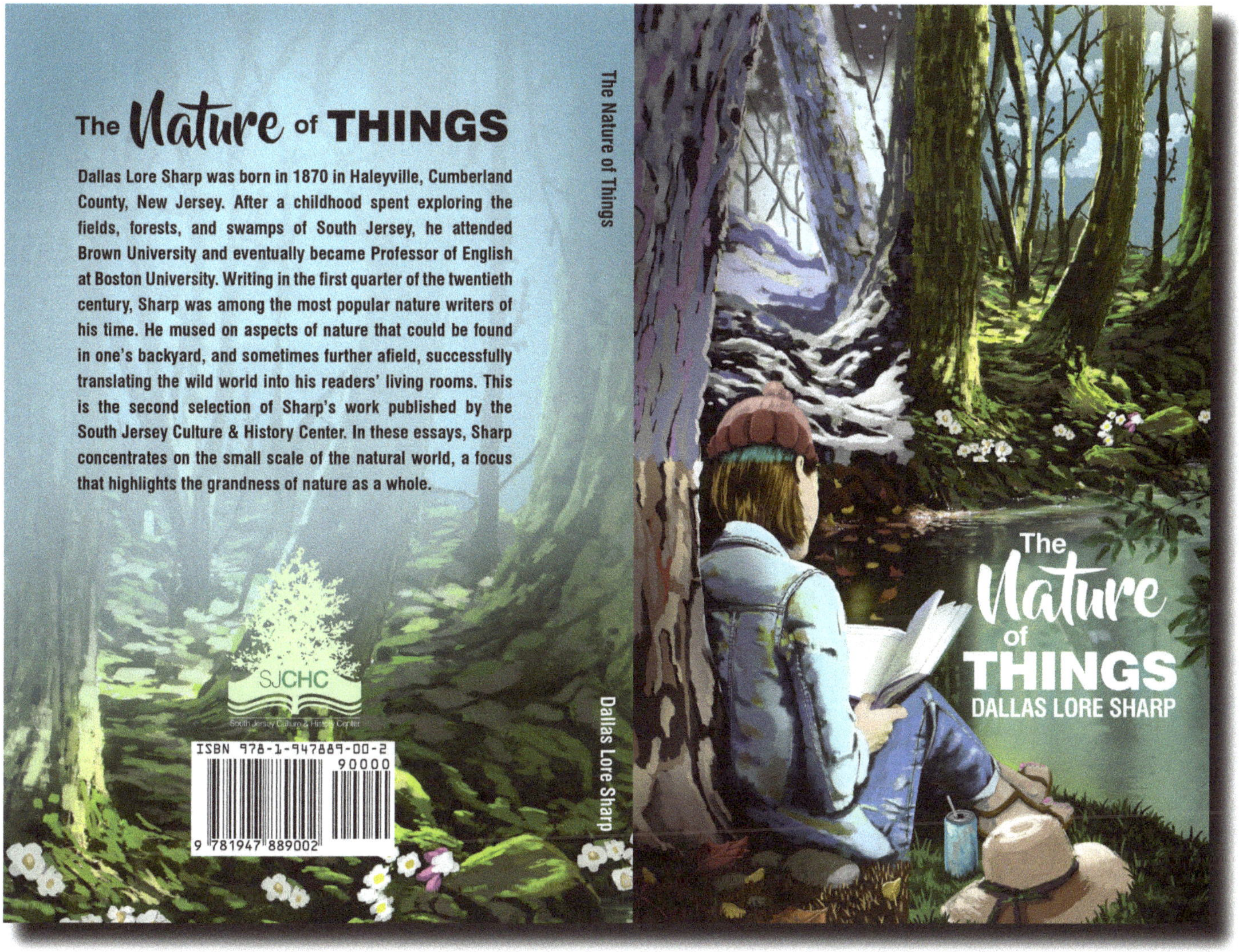

The Nature of THINGS

Dallas Lore Sharp was born in 1870 in Haleyville, Cumberland County, New Jersey. After a childhood spent exploring the fields, forests, and swamps of South Jersey, he attended Brown University and eventually became Professor of English at Boston University. Writing in the first quarter of the twentieth century, Sharp was among the most popular nature writers of his time. He mused on aspects of nature that could be found in one's backyard, and sometimes further afield, successfully translating the wild world into his readers' living rooms. This is the second selection of Sharp's work published by the South Jersey Culture & History Center. In these essays, Sharp concentrates on the small scale of the natural world, a focus that highlights the grandness of nature as a whole.

SJCHC

South Jersey Culture & History Center

ISBN 978-1-947889-00-2

9 781947 889002 90000

The Nature of Things Dallas Lore Sharp

The Nature of THINGS

DALLAS LORE SHARP

***The Nature of Things* by Dallas Lore Sharp**

Publication of our second volume of nature essays by South Jersey native Dallas Lore Sharp has been delayed by difficulties arising from the recent pandemic. A follow-up to *Seasons* (2015), *The Nature of Things* is a selection of essays from Sharp's *The Whole Year Round*. Born in 1870 in Haleyville, Cumberland County, New Jersey, Sharp concentrates upon the small scale of the natural world, a focus that highlights the interrelatedness of the world around us. The essays are written in an engaging and often moving style.

180 pages, paperback.
ISBN: 978-1-947889-00-2.

Available soon at Second Time Books, Mount Laurel, and on Amazon.

SOUTH JERSEY
HORSE
RESCUE

South Jersey Horse Rescue

Amanda Clark and Sarahjane Hehre

Ellen Strack has been in love with horses since she was twelve; she had her own horse as a child; and then she found out about horse slaughter. Since 2010, with the help of many, many volunteers, including Bette Ann Feldeisen, Betty Morgan and Megan Alyssa Carovillano, Ellen has come to the rescue of horses whose reality resembles the backdrop of horror films. With the help of donations, fundraisers, and many volunteers, Ellen maintains the South Jersey Horse Rescue, a safe haven for horses in desperate situations. Located in Weekstown, New Jersey, with an Egg Harbor City mailing address, the South Jersey Horse Rescue takes in horses of all kinds, as well as ponies, donkeys, and mules. The Rescue is a nonprofit 501(c)(3) that rehabilitates and, if possible, finds new homes for horses.

Many people are not aware of the struggles that horses can face. To urban and suburban families, with no equine experience, horses are beautiful animals, seen through a car window, grazing in green fields. The truth is that horses are still a source of income for many people. They are used for racing, summer camp riding, performance (barrel racing, jumping), or to sustain a livelihood as Amish people do (plowing fields, pulling carts). As horses age, they lose their value; when they lose their value, they often end up in an auction and if they are not bid on, they are shipped from auction to auction, wearing them down and putting them at risk to be bought cheaply by horse meat brokers.

What is the fate of horses whose loving owners die, become ill, divorce or go bankrupt? Any number of life-changing events for humans can place a horse at risk as well. As Ellen explains, these graceful animals may find their way to auction houses. Equine kill shelters are illegal in the United States, but not elsewhere. Auction houses sell horses to the highest bidder, by the pound, and too many horses can be found on trains or trucks going to Mexico and Canada where they can be legally killed, their meat shipped to destinations where it is popular such as Europe and Asia. Attend a horse auction and too often you will find abused, blind, three-legged, malnourished, pregnant, diseased or abandoned horses, all for sale for slaughter.

Bette Feldeisen was inspired to help save vulnerable horses when she met up with Ellen Strack eight years ago and learned of the dangers that awaited too many auction horses. She also learned of the network of horse rescue facilities, stretching across the US, where often very badly treated horses have the chance to recuperate, be retrained, and be adopted.

Ellen and Bette, along with other volunteers and supportive donors, help to provide a safe and nurturing environment that offers quality of life to often discarded horses. They provide them the opportunity to gain their health, adjust within a safe setting, and, hopefully, find a new loving home. With each successful adoption, the South Jersey Horse Rescue keeps in touch with the adopting families and continues to help any way it can. It is a labor of love.

How You Can Help

The South Jersey Horse Rescue is a non-profit organization that depends upon volunteers, fundraising, and donations. Volunteers receive orientation to help them better understand the duties of the facility and the necessary work ethic. They learn about the sometimes fragile psychological state of incoming horses. They help with feeding, training, riding, and cleaning the horses and their areas. They spend time with the horses to help them regain trust and feel comfortable around humans. In addition, Ellen and Bette host groups such as the Boys and Girls Club, Big Brother, and Boy and Girl Scouts to help bring awareness to their cause and to promote safe animal treatment. Ellen also paints portraits of animals and humans, which she sells at low cost, giving all profits to the Horse Rescue.

The South Jersey Horse Rescue sources as many products locally as possible and recycles or composts the majority of their refuse, sustaining a healthy environment and remaining as close to zero waste as possible. Please check out their Facebook page and website (below) to learn more. Donate, adopt and/or look for options to volunteer or host your own group at the Rescue Center.

South Jersey Horse Rescue
5745 Pleasant Mills Road, Egg Harbor City, New Jersey 08215
(609) 965-0274
Website: https://www.southjerseyhorserescue.com/
Facebook: https://www.facebook.com/SJABHR/
Email: Southjerseyhorserescue@comcast.net

About the Authors

Amanda Clark is a Junior at Stockton University studying Literature with a concentration in Creative Writing. With some experience in editing, in the process of self publishing her first book, and planning to study abroad at Trinity College, Dublin, Amanda is excited to see what her future plans have to offer and hopes to use her platform to promote awareness for mental health and helping the environment.

Sarahjane Hehre is a Senior at Stockton University studying Literature with a minor in Women, Gender and Sexuality. With a few editing and writing internship experiences, Sarahjane would like to further her literature study with an aspiring focus in Environmental and Marine sciences. She plans to research, write and bring awareness to current and future environmental issues and solutions.

Call for Articles

The South Jersey Culture & History Center at Stockton University publishes twice yearly issues of *SoJourn*. We actively seek community members, avocational historians, and scholars to contribute essays on topics related to South Jersey. Illustrations to accompany these articles will be a plus. Articles should be written for laypersons who are interested and curious about South Jersey topics, but do not necessarily have expertise in the areas covered. Potential authors should check SJCHC's website for a link to a simplified style sheet guide for article preparation—www.stockton.edu/sjchc/—or just follow the style in this issue. Journal editors will be happy to guide any would-be authors. In certain instances, Stockton editing interns may be assigned to help research topics and/or assist authors with writing.

Sample topics might include:

Biographical sketches of important but forgotten local people; the development or succession of a community's roads, bridges or buildings; local transportation (focused by mode, area or era) and what changes it wrought in the served communities; history of community businesses and industries (wineries, garment factories, agriculture, boat building, clamming, etc.); old school houses, old hotels, or meeting halls; narrative descriptions of local geographical features; essays concerned with folklore, music, arts; and reviews of new local interest publications. Photo essays and old photograph and postcard reproductions are welcome with applicable captions. In short, if a South Jersey topic interests you, it will likely interest *SoJourn*'s readers.

Parameters for submissions:

• Submissions must pertain to topics bounded within the eight southernmost counties of New Jersey (Burlington & Ocean Counties and south)
• Manuscripts should be approximately 3,000–4,000 words long (5 to 7 pages of single-spaced text and 9 to 12 pages including images)
• Manuscripts should conform to the *SoJourn* style sheet, available here: https://blogs.stockton.edu/sjchc/sojourn-style-sheet/
• Manuscripts, if at all possible, should be submitted in digital format (Word- or pdf-formatted documents preferred)
• Images should be submitted as high-resolution tiff- or jpeg-formatted files (editors can assist with digital conversion of photos if necessary). 300 dpi resolution, or higher, preferred
• Complete and appropriate citations printed as endnotes should be employed (see style sheet). If using Word, please use its automated endnote function
• Original submissions only. Copyright licenses for all images must be obtained by the author or should be copyright-free figures and/or figures in the public domain
• If essays are accepted, authors should submit a short 50 to 100 word autobiographical statement
• Articles need to be more than just a chronology of the given topic. The author should be able to properly contextualize the subject by answering such questions as: a) why is this important?; b) what is the impact on the local or regional history? and c) how does it compare to similar events/personages/changes/processes in other localities?

Call for submissions:

Submissions for winter issues are due before September 1; for summer issues, January 15.

Send inquiries or submissions to Thomas.Kinsella@stockton.edu or Paul.Schopp@stockton.edu.

The iron star used as section separator above, and at the conclusion of several articles, is part of a small collection of ironwork salvaged from the hay barn on the property of Buzby's general store in Chatsworth, New Jersey. The barn had fallen into disrepair and Marilyn Schmidt, who restored the Buzby property in 1999, had the structure disassembled. The cedar boards of the barn were repurposed to rebuild the Buzby outhouse in 2001. This ironwork is available for inspection in Special Collections, the Bjork Library, Stockton University.

Train Stations of South Jersey

Cover Images, *SoJourn* 5.2

Paul W. Schopp

Front Cover (clockwise, from top left)

Woodstown Station, Salem County

The New Jersey Legislature incorporated the Woodstown & Swedesboro Railroad in March 1871 to construct a line between the end of the Swedesboro Railroad (completed 1869) and the Salem Railroad (completed 1863) at Riddleton. Construction of the line did not begin for another eleven years, in 1882, and then built under the auspices of the West Jersey Railroad. The Woodstown station complex, placed in service during February 1883, included the passenger depot as well as a freight station, complete with a raised platform to facilitate loading and unloading from freight cars and baggage cars. The shell of the passenger station still survives in derelict condition on the old Sickler farm, located at the Route 40 – Commissioners Road intersection. It was removed from the railroad right-of-way sometime after 1950, when passenger service ceased operations.

Williamstown Station, Gloucester County

The Williamstown Railroad received its charter in March 1871 to construct a rail line between Atco, on the Camden & Atlantic Railroad, and the line's namesake to principally serve Thomas Bodine's glassworks. The railroad reached Williamstown two years later. Grading work to extend the line to Glassboro was accomplished but rail laying was not completed before the company entered bankruptcy in 1881. At the October 1883 foreclosure sale, the Philadelphia & Reading Railroad and its then subsidiary, the Central Railroad of New Jersey, acquired the company and its line. The new owners reincorporated the railroad as the Williamstown & Delaware River Railroad and the Central made plans to extend the line to Penns Grove and establish a ferry service there, but the extension failed to materialize. In this view of Williamstown station, the gable of one building in the glassworks can been seen on the extreme right behind the boxcar.

South Vineland Station, Cumberland County

The West Jersey Railroad, chartered in 1853, completed its line to Glassboro in 1861 and then diverted to Bridgeton, rather than to Millville. To gain railroad service, Millville industrialists incorporated the Millville & Glassboro Railroad in 1859 to connect with the West Jersey at Glassboro. The M&G traversed the area that would become Millville and provided Charles K. Landis with the impetus needed to establish his ideal utopian city. With the railroad in place, Landis platted his new community in 1861. Two satellite settlements soon developed: North and South Vineland. The latter location first appeared in the West Jersey schedule in 1867, suggesting the station had been constructed that year. The depot continued to serve the traveling public until November 1938, when the railroad sold the original station to a Main Road farmer and replaced it with a small shelter for waiting passengers.

Absecon Station, Atlantic County

Incorporated in March 1852, the Camden & Atlantic Railroad completed its route from Coopers Point, Camden, to Atlantic City in July 1854, passing through many communities across South Jersey, including Absecon. It appears the railroad constructed this station during the 1860s. It remained in service until about 1940, when the railroad elevated the tracks through the community to eliminate grade crossings as ordered by the state's Public Utility Commission. The frame station, pictured here and standing on the east side of the railroad and south side of Station Avenue, was demolished as part of the reconstruction work.

Tuckahoe Station, Cape May County

The Philadelphia & Reading Railroad, parent company of the Atlantic City Railroad, built Tuckahoe Station in 1894, following its acquisition of the South Jersey Railroad, successor to the Philadelphia & Sea Shore Railroad. Tuckahoe served as a junction point between the route to Ocean City and Sea Isle and the line that extended to Cape May with a branch to Wildwood. The P&R contracted with the Philadelphia architectural firm of Wilson Brothers to design the Tuckahoe Station, which featured a passenger waiting room, trainmaster's office, and crew quarters on the first floor and bunk rooms for crews on the second floor. The station complex included a freight station and an interlocking tower to control the junction between the two branches. In 1984, the station became listed in the National Register of Historic Places and in recent years, the building underwent complete restoration.

Ashland Station, Camden County

The unincorporated community of Ashland straddles the present-day Cherry Hill-Voorhees boundary. Prior to the construction of the Camden & Atlantic Railroad in the early 1850s, the place name Ashland did not exist on the landscape. When the railroad established a station at the Evesham Road crossing, the company named it Ashland. This c. 1907 summer view of Ashland Station is looking towards Atlantic City with a crowd of beach-going revelers waiting for the train to take them to the sun, sand, and waves of America's playground.

Rear Cover (clockwise, from top left)

Island Heights Station, Ocean County

Prior to 1878, Island Heights, situated on the north shore of Toms River, served as farmland. In that year, however, a group of ministers and businessmen led by the Rev. Jacob Graw, formed the Island Heights Association and established a Methodist camp meeting there. Four years later, the Pennsylvania Railroad incorporated the Island Heights Railroad Company and immediately began building trestling and a movable bridge over the Toms River, completing it in 1884. The 1.16-mile line extended from the Philadelphia & Long Branch Railroad over to the island. As shown in this view, the station building stood on pilings along the trestle with a wooden walkway leading to the fast land. Passenger service ended in 1931 and three years later, the railroad removed the trestling, bridge, and station.

Bayside Station, Cumberland County

When completed, the Vineland Railway extended from Atsion to the Delaware Bay at what would become Bayside. Originally platted as Bay City, Bayside featured a railroad car float slip, but the service never started. The float operations only lasted for a couple of years and nothing materialized of the city planned there. Bayside included an elevated pier, warehouse space, a station, fishery equipment storage, and seafood packing facilities. By the early twentieth century, one roundtrip accommodation train served Bayside, shown in this view. The pier burned in 1914 and passenger service ended to Bayside in 1923. The Central Railroad of New Jersey, who assumed control in 1878, formally abandoned the line in 1936.

Millville Station, Cumberland County

The Millville and Glassboro Railroad completed its line to Glassboro in 1860. To complete the route to Cape May, the Cape May and Millville Railroad formed in 1863. The M&G began construction in 1862, knowing the CM&M would become a reality. The Millville passenger station included a commodious waiting room and a baggage room. Across the tracks from the passenger depot stood the freight station with a raised platform to make shipment handling easier. From 1906 until 1949, the Millville Station handled electric train service to Camden as well as regular steam and diesel passenger trains.

Goshen Station, Cape May County

When the South Jersey Railroad completed its route to Cape May in 1893–94, the company established a station for the village of Goshen located approximately two miles from the community. Known as Goshen Station, the passenger depot included a block station and train order signal and, across the tracks, a diminutive freight station and elevated platform. Note the oil lamps used to light the waiting platform.

Atlantic City Station, Atlantic County

Since its completion in 1854, the Camden & Atlantic Railroad became the route of choice for traveling to Atlantic City, even after the upstart narrow gauge Philadelphia & Atlantic City became a competitor in 1877. Known as the "Old Reliable," the C&A provided a safe and convenient way to reach the coast. With a swelling crowd expected for the nation's Centennial Celebration to be held in Philadelphia, the C&A expected a crush of people wishing to escape the urban heat by traveling to the shore. This anticipation caused the C&A to build a new and modern terminal in Atlantic City during the fall and winter of 1875–76. Located near the intersection of Atlantic and South Carolina avenue, the station remained in service until the newly formed Pennsylvania-Reading Seashore Lines erected their Union Station in 1934, whereupon the railroad razed the former C&A station.

Elmer Station, Salem County

Upon reaching Glassboro during construction, the West Jersey Railroad chose to build its line to Bridgeton rather than Millville, and arrived at the former place in 1861, passing through Elmer. In 1863, interests in Salem desired to build a connecting railroad in 1863 between Elmer and Salem to provide rail service to the latter place. The Elmer passenger and freight stations sat in the crotch of the two converging railroads and shipped vast quantities of farm produce and truck, including potatoes, as shown in this view. After the railroad discontinued using the station, it was relocated to Route 40 outside of Elmer and served as a restaurant named the Country Kitchen, but within the last few years, the station suffered demolition.

Atsion Station, Burlington County

The Raritan & Delaware Bay Railroad reached the Pine Barrens community of Atsion in 1863 and built a branch to connect to the Camden & Atlantic at Jackson, near Atco. By 1870, the company had constructed a combination freight and passenger station at Atsion since the Vineland Railway had connected its track to the R&DB/New Jersey Southern line. The station remained in service with the Central Railroad of New Jersey, successor to the New Jersey Southern in 1878, until the railroad discontinued the depot in 1949. A local farmer purchased the building and relocated it to his fields for use as a pickers' shack. In the 1980s, a florist acquired the dilapidated station and used it as part of his display at the Philadelphia Flower Show and that was the last time the building was seen.

Pleasantville Station, Atlantic County

In 1879, the West Jersey Railroad, lacking a route into Atlantic City, incorporated the West Jersey & Atlantic Railroad to build a rail line from Newfield, Gloucester County, to the seaside resort. The railroad completed the line in 1880, and the West Jersey offered yet a third railroad route into America's Playground. In 1906, the Pennsylvania Railroad, parent of the succeeding West Jersey & Seashore, electrified the WJ&A to operate high-speed electric trains between the Camden ferries, Atlantic City, and also to Millville. Pleasantville Station became an important stop for the electric cars and the Atlantic and Suburban trolley cars provided connecting service at the station. Electric train service to Atlantic City ended in 1931 and the Pennsylvania-Reading Seashore Lines eventually discontinued its Pleasantville station and demolition occurred sometime during the late 1950s or early 1960s.

Inset: Train approaching Chatsworth Station

A Central Railroad of New Jersey express train approaches Chatsworth Station in the early twentieth century. The Raritan & Delaware Bay Railroad first established a stop named Shamong at this location in 1862 and constructed the first station four years later. In 1876, the New Jersey Southern Railroad built a new station here. The station underwent a name change in 1893. It was renamed Chatsworth to coincide with the creation of the Chatsworth Club, an upscale private club for the wealthy bon vivants of New York, Philadelphia, and elsewhere. The owners initially used the White Horse Hotel until the clubhouse was ready. The club life lasted only about 10 years or so before the Burlington County Sheriff sold the clubhouse and its grounds under a court order in 1907. About four years later, the club burned to the ground. To accommodate the crowds using the trains on the CNJ, the railroad erected a new station in 1897. The railroad closed its agency there and sold the station in 1952. The new owners moved it from the right-of-way to a nearby location and converted it into a house, which it remains today.

www.ingramcontent.com/pod-product-compliance
Lightning Source LLC
LaVergne TN
LVHW060644110826
845147LV00018B/1037

* 9 7 8 1 9 4 7 8 8 9 0 4 0 *